We Believe in One God

We Believe in One God

The experience of God in Christianity and Islam

Edited by

Annemarie Schimmel
and Abdoldjavad Falatūri

Preface by

Kenneth Cragg

A Crossroad Book · The Seabury Press · New York

1979
The Seabury Press
815 Second Avenue
New York, N.Y. 1017
Originally published as *Glauben an den einen Gott: Menschliche Gotteserfahrung im Christentum und im Islam.*

Translated by Gerald Blaczszak, S.J., and Annemarie Schimmel

Printed in the United States of America

Library of Congress Cataloging in Publication Data
Main entry under title:
We believe in one god.
Translation of Glauben an den einen Gott; with one essay substituted.
1. Islam—Addresses, essays, lectures. 2. Theology—Addresses, essays, lectures. I. Schimmel, Annemarie. II. Falaturi, Abdoldjavad, 1925-
BR20.G5513 297 79-2457 ISBN 0-8164-0451-8

Contents

Preface

A 'symposium', to the Greeks, was quite simply a drinking party. The term in current academic usage has become much less convivial and therefore the more sober. In documented form such occasions are often hard to evaluate, if only because the immediacy of the encounter of kindred minds is lost in the record. The Papers read at the November 1974 Symposium organized by Oratio Dominica are no exception. They offer a variety of assessments and interpretations in areas that are central to the spiritual and intellectual converse of Islam and Christianity today and so to the concerns that belong with the integrity of faith in disciples and scholars in each tradition. The editors have discharged their task in a way that merits the careful attention of a wide readership.

Two broad considerations emerge. The first is the relative isolation of German-speaking 'theological orientalism' from its English-speaking counterpart. The situation is largely mutual and no doubt the responsibility for it also. That it should be so makes the English edition of *Glauben an den einen Gott: Menschliche Gotteserfahrung im Christentum und im Islam* the more timely and welcome.

The other, and much more vital, reflection has to do with 'radical' monotheism, which, as the whole text indicates, is the theme of themes between us, the theme which controls all others, and both divides and unites Muslims and Christians. 'Radical', like many another label when in vogue, is liable to be elusive or ambiguous. *Non Deus nisi Deus solus* we would all say. But is monotheism truly 'radical' merely by being insistent credally? If it is conceptually numerical will it be radical enough?

In comprehensive context there is no finer, no truer, definition of *islām* (Islam) than Martin Luther's plea: 'Let God be God'. Essentially, of course, nothing prevents Him being God. God He is: in sovereignty altogether final and alone. Yet, in an undeviating worship, it is ours to *let* Him be God. Idolatry demonstrates dramatically how that acknowledged worship may be withheld from Him, misdirected in *Shirk*, alienated to pseudo-deities, those non-entities which *ẓulm* and *kufr* substitute for God. Were that idolatry negligible, permissible, innocuous, there would of course be no point in the Prophet's mission. That mission on behalf of the divine Unity means that the divine rule is something we have it in us to ignore or to deny. So a 'radical', prophetic monotheism will not merely assert but will 'avail' that Unity. Such is the sense of *Tauḥīd* as the intensive, reflexive form—not merely to propose that God is One but to demand that He be unrivalled in the heart and in the world.

That 'letting God be God' is bound up with the whole nature of creation and the creation of nature. In these, again, we both believe. But the Creator cannot will the creature and then be as if without him. 'Almighty' and 'Creator' will be contradictory terms if, by the former, we mean 'wholly unconditioned'. The divine *kenosis* implicit in creation, and in law for the creation, and in human *khilāfah*, or 'dominion', must have its due place in our understanding of *Allāhu akbar*. That 'God is One' is credal statement: that 'God *may be* all in all' is realized *islām*. A 'radical' monotheism will always see 'realization' as a more final task than statement.

Here, surely, is the ultimate locus of our mutual thinking. Time, the changing world, man's gathering technology, our global economic inequalities, secularization—all these with their tests of personal maturity and religious institutions come within the single question of the rule of God and of man's being within it. Have Christians, either in theology or in friendship, yet sufficiently realized how integral to their own thinking are the essential implications of Islam? Have Muslims yet seen how integral to their concern for an adequate monotheism, in faith and fact, are the Christian criteria of God as love, vulnerable to man in evil and, thereby self-consistently ultimate in redemption and grace?

These are the questions between us, squarely rooted in the theme of God, on which all secondary issues depend, and to which all debate about inspiration, authority, tradition and *ijmā'*, must for ever return.

How self-conscious we still are about our identities! Dictionaries somehow confirm the disparity of languages even in the enterprise of bringing them together! Can we not hope that sometime, somewhere, we might somehow be so aware of God, *Subḥāna wa Ta'ālā*, that we might forget we are partisans of His theologies? The day may still be remote, like the day when Christians can freely share the precincts of Mecca. But if it ever comes the sort of patient scholarship these papers offer will have been contributory.

Kenneth Cragg

Foreword

For more than a thousand years Muslims and Christians have tried to develop ideas about their respective faiths. During the Middle Ages the first interreligious disputations took place at the courts of Muslim rulers: for instance, in Baghdad, and in the Islamic West. Politically, Christians were on the defensive at the time, and in a difficult position when dealing with Islam. A religion that had appeared after Christianity could, for them, be nothing but a caricature, an evil and corrupt imitation of Christian truth. Muḥammad, the Prophet of Islam, was described as an impostor, a sensualist and deceiver, and even as the Anti-Christ.

Muslims, on the other hand, could react towards Christians with greater ease, since the Koran termed both Christians and Jews *ahl al-kitāb*, 'those who possess a book'; Jesus was venerated as the last great messenger of God before Muḥammad, as 'a spirit from God' (Sura 4/69), and soon became a model for the ascetics and mystics of Islam. Yet the German Romantic Novalis, in his novel *Heinrich von Ofterdingen*, makes his Muslim heroine Zulima complain that the Christians persecuted the Muslims, while 'we, full of devotion, venerate the person of Jesus, whom we accept as a prophet'. Even today the alleged tomb of Mary near Izmir in Turkey is a place of pilgrimage for Muslims as well as for Christians.

During the Middle Ages religious prejudices and the political situation were impediments to greater understanding between the two religions, both of which were heirs to the 'Abrahamic' tradition. Muslim theologians studied the gospels in order to refute the divinity of Christ and, since, the Koran denies the crucifixion, accused Christians of falsifying Jesus's original message. They detected contradictions in the four gospels, and vehemently opposed the doctrine of the Trinity, which seemed to contradict the pure monotheism of Islam. Christian theologians, on the other hand, disparaged Muslims and misunderstood the Koran. Only a few of them reached a deeper understanding of the ethical values of a religion that was generally described as utterly sensual. The Catalan thinker Ramon Lull (d. 1316), in spite of his missionary attempts in North Africa, was one of the handful of Christians who discovered the Islamic mystical tradition, on which he drew in some of his works. In his great novel *Blanquerna* Lull brings together the representatives of the three Abrahamic religions in a friendly disputation, and the closing section, *The Book of the Lover and the Beloved*, relies largely on Islamic mystical sources, part of which he translated verbatim. Nicholas of Cusa is among those who tried to study Islam and its holy book without his contemporaries' general aversion to it. There were new outbreaks of hatred against the 'Muhammadans' during the sixteenth and seventeenth centuries, when Austria (and hence Germany) was threatened by the Ottoman armies; the *Türkenlieder,* popular songs composed during the period, reflect the general feelings about the detested 'Muhammadans' as much as some of the publications concerning the Ottoman Empire, or some of Lohenstein's bloodthirsty 'Turkish' tragedies.

At the same time, however, travellers to the East returned with a different picture of the cultural achievements of the Muslims, and the Enlightenment offered wider horizons to the West.

In the late eighteenth century a new, scholarly interest in the Arabic language emerged in several European countries. The Prophet Muḥammad even appears in some books as an inaugurator of a 'more rational' religion. The German dramatist

Lessing revived the motif of the friendly competition of the three Abrahamic religions in his play *Nathan der Weise*, and reconfirmed the positive image of Sultan Saladin, to whom even Dante had assigned a comparatively comfortable place in the Otherworld. From 1800 onwards European scholars began to study the sources of the Islamic religion and history in greater depth, and in spite of some extreme, critical studies of Muḥammad, a slightly more conciliatory attitude toward Islam developed—first pronounced in Germany by Goethe in his *West-Östlicher Divan*, and in Britain by Carlyle in *On Heroes and Hero Worship* (his chapter on Muḥammad is still quoted by Muslims to prove the greatness of the Prophet).

The growing interest in and knowledge of Islamic subjects in the West appeared at a time when the Islamic countries had reached a certain ebb in their political and, largely, cultural life and coincided with the expansion of western colonial powers from North Africa to Muslim India and Indonesia; they were bound to call forth violent reactions from Muslims. These tensions affected the possibility of a new dialogue, as previous difficulties had during the Middle Ages. The chances of any real dialogue became more complicated as more Muslim intellectuals were trained in Western universities, and returned with changed ideas. They were often completely alienated from their religious past so that they seemed have little in common with large non-westernized, traditional circles in their own countries. Yet, even in a 'laicist' country like Turkey adherence to Islam as a religion, though perhaps not as a system regulating every moment of life, was amazingly strong, and practically unshakable even in those who seemed outwardly completely westernized.

During the five years while one of the undersigned was teaching history of religions to students of the Faculty of Islamic Theology in Ankara, she was often faced with the problems which were foremost in the minds of young Turkish Muslim theologians—who were deeply rooted in their pious traditions in spite of the official secularism—when they had to deal with Christianity. She witnessed their desire for a clear picture of the development of the

Christian churches and denominations, which seemed so strange to them. One experience, however, was rewarding: the best common ground of understanding was the world of religious experience, the faith in the one God, Creator, Sustainer, and Judge. Dogmatic differences notwithstanding, Christian and Muslim could meet by exchanging prayers or religious hymns.

The attitude of the second Vatican Council to the non-Christian religions has offered a greater possibility of understanding than ever before. Professor Anawati, OP, one of the leading Islamicists of our day, has correctly remarked the extreme importance for Christian–Muslim relations of the conciliar declaration that the God of Islam is the One, Living, Self-Subsistent, Merciful and Omnipotent God, Creator of Heaven and earth.

On the basis of that conviction the Oratio Dominica foundation held a symposium in November 1974 to clarify some of the issues in Muslim–Christian dialogue. Christian and Muslim theologians of various denominations, as well as orientalists, were invited to the meeting. The papers read there appear here in English translation; one article has been added. In it, Professor Falatūri discusses the possibility of experiencing God in Islam in spite of its strict monotheism, and introduces (as he does in his other paper) the mystically-tinged philosophy of life of Shia Iran (a world view introduced to western readers mainly by Henri Corbin). Smail, Balić, on the other hand, represents traditional orthodox Sunni Islam; his attitude is possibly more clearly defined in that he comes from the periphery of the Islamic world and a minority Muslim community. His valuable contribution to the discussion of Jesus in the Koran (so often repeated by western scholars in the last few decades) does not admit of any mystical or popular interpretation of the figure of Jesus, but states the Koranic facts with uncompromising clarity.

Unfortunately, Hamid Algar's paper was not available in its English original version and his views could not be included in full. Professor Algar, a British Muslim, discussed the problems of modernization and secularization in the Muslim world, and with extreme acerbity criticized all attempts to wean away Muslims from the word of the Koran and the tradition of the Prophet. Professor Algar stressed the fact that he was expressing the attitude of faithful traditionalist circles, without claiming to offer a 'scholarly' discourse. He highlighted the essential unity of Islam reflected in the unity of the worldly and the other worldly spheres, and manifested in the amazing uniformity of Islamic civilization from West Africa to the East Indies. Secularization means the separation of *dīn* and *daula*, religion and state, which comprises *inter alia* the introduction into Muslim countries of western legal codes instead of the God-given laws of the *sharīʿa*. *The activities* of Christian missionaries are said to have served the process of secularization by undermining the unity of Islam, just as the non-Muslim minorities, such as Christian Arabs, Armenians, Copts, and so on, were the spearheads of secularizing movements. Algar rightly said that the westernization of Turkey has resulted in hardly any change of western attitudes to the country. Age-old memories of the Turkish wars linger on and prevent western nations from accepting Turkey fully as one of them. The personality cult, as is evident in modern Islamic countries (Iran, Nasser's Egypt, and so on), belongs here as much as the cult of nationalism (Iqbal, the Indo-Muslim thinker, called patriotism 'a subtle form of idolatry'). Here there is a danger of Communism and of attempts to change religion into ideology. Those exposed to such dangers may refuse to believe in a profound experience of the Divine. Another problem of secularization is the transformation of Islamic cities which, in response to the needs of the population and the prescriptions of religion, have become nondescript modern conurbations. Professor Algar discussed the various suggestions offered by western thinkers and Orientalists to help Muslims 'modernize' their lives, but refuted them all as interfering with the one and unique revelation of God as contained in the Koran. Every Muslim, even in a modern state, still has the possibility of realizing the commandments of Islam—prayer, fasting, pilgrimage, and so on—in his own life, of following the noble example of the Prophet, and of directing his whole life towards God, the sole object of worship.

Professor Algar's remarks revealed the wide gap between the

traditional Muslim view and that of the Orientalists who, like Professor Paret in his contribution, try to lead Muslims towards modernization by indicating steps that have been successful in Christianity—such as reformation and, lately, demythologization.

On the other hand, during the symposium Christian views of secularization and the person of Jesus in modern exegesis showed the Muslims various ways of interpreting Jesus and his message in our time. The discussions of the visible tensions between Christianity and Islam, but also of the differences of interpretation within each of the two great religions, were remarkably frank, and thought-provoking.

Since Islamic ideas were presented by scholars and theologians who were steeped in the mystical tradition, a paper on the mystical piety of Christianity might have seemed desirable. The experience of God in Thomas Aquinas or Luther, Origen or Calvin, in Greek Orthodox mystical poetry or among the Quakers, are topics that were also relevant to the central theme. The discussion could have gone on to the Muslim reformers of the eighteenth century, or the modernists of the mid-twentieth century. But the innumerable aspects of each religion could not be exhausted, or even touched on, in one symposium. The most important task was to clarify the issues, and to reach the conclusion that, in spite of outward dogmatic differences, there is already a common basis of religious experience. In fact, a deeply religious Christian and a very devout Muslim probably have a more solid foundation of mutual understanding than modernized or excessively secularized members of Christian and Muslim communities.

In this perspective, the different approaches of the participants in the symposium on which this book is based, and hence the book itself, may be seen as an important contribution to better understanding between the two religions, and as an attempt to reach the ultimate reality, the source of faith, which underlies the various manifestations of religion in time and space.

Cambridge, Mass., 1977 — *Annemarie Schimmel*
Cologne, 1977 — *Abdoldjavad Falatūri*

We Believe in One God

The Image of Jesus in Contemporary Islamic Theology

Smail Balić

If theology is discourse about God, then Islamic theology makes no assertions concerning Jesus Christ. Islam rules out any incursion of the human into the sphere of the divine. One cannot speak of any experience of God in the sense of Christian theology.

In Islam Jesus has a thoroughly human dimension. Only his unusual birth sets him above ordinary mortals. Because of the very nature of Muslim theology, no relationship can be set up between the person of Christ and Muslim theology.

In contrast to biblically-oriented Christian theology, which is concerned not simply with God, but with a personal union between God and man, Islam would dispel from the believer's mind any thought of a human share in the divine uniqueness. If we remember that Christian theologians are usually theologians precisely because they believe in Jesus Christ and, in a particular way, in God,[1] we can see how distant the points of departure of the two theological systems are from one another.

The chasm seems to be unbridgeable if we think of some modern theologians who attempt (misguidedly, in the perspective of Christian orthodoxy) to dismiss the idea of God entirely. If Jesus is so interpreted that we no longer refer to the concept of God as found in revelation, then Christianity and Islam have nothing at all in common. Christians and Muslims can agree only on a belief in God who brought forth and sustains creation. Nothing, not even Jesus, whom even Islam elevates above other mortals, can replace this fundamental religious value, namely, belief in God, the creator.

In Islam Jesus, like all other prophets, is reduced to human dimensions. Therefore, in Muslim discussion, Jesus does not possess the importance which is his in Christianity. In the Koran Jesus is simply a subject of the history of prophets. In any case, the interpretation of this history is not uniform. While the older Koran commentators accept it as a transmission of actual events, more modern exegetes (ᶜAbdarrāziq, Djozo, Korkut, and others) ascribe to it a literary and pedagogical function of an auxiliary nature. They appeal to the fact that the Koran itself calls special attention to the parenetic-literary and aesthetic intention of some of the stories of the prophets. For example, the story of the Egyptian Joseph is qualified as 'the most beautiful tale'.[2]

In general, these groups of Koranic passages consist of sidelights, fragments and intimations. There are no complete accounts. All this indicates that they are intended to play only a secondary rôle in the total plan of the Koran. To a certain extent, they are a subculture within the Koranic world of thought and feelings.

According to this interpretation, which is increasingly accepted nowadays, the tales of the prophets are a sort of literary material designed to while away the evening hours, and at the same time to serve as a basis for discussion with other revealed religions. What is important in these stories, according to this view, is not so much their contents but their effect as aids in strengthening the faith of a particular audience. They incite and stimulate the pious mind. The hero is an image for imitation (*uswa ḥasana*). In his human dimensions, therefore, he must appeal to the listener.

The Koran has its own versions of certain biblical stories. Their presence suggests that it was not Muḥammad's intention to deal theologically with the content of the stories of the prophets. Islam did not arise out of the history of a convenant with God, as is the case with Judaism.[3] An intimate connexion between God and man based on interaction in history is unknown to Islam. Therefore the stories of the prophets rank second or third at best in the Islamic doctrinal system. The demarcation-line from the sphere of faith (*'aqā'id, i'tiqādāt*) is very sharp. These stories are to a large extent understood as legends. They have no direct function in the active faith of Muslims.

That is also the reason why the Islamic authorities on the Scriptures have never seriously concerned themselves with Christology. When Ali Merad explains this as a 'grande discrétion' in order to avoid sterile controversies with Christians, it should be remarked that this 'great reserve' is possible only because no issues of high priority in regard to faith are involved. The fact that the chapter of *Jesus* belongs to the 'domaine de l'Inconnaissable' (*ghayb*) is a less decisive, yet contributing factor.[4] What aṭ-Ṭabarī (d. 923), Ibn an-Nadīm (d. 995 or 998), ash-Shahrastānī (d. 1153) and other historians and scholars of religion had to say about Jesus is merely information of a modest and summary nature. It is primarily Christian missionaries, or certain Orientalists who are either themselves theologians, or who are well disposed to Christian theology, who overestimate the rôle of Jesus in the Koran. They are misled by the way of understanding Jesus which they retain from their Christian Tradition. It is no surprise that, under such circumstances, they arrive at false conclusions and evaluations. Heikki Räisänen, a Finnish New Testament scholar who wrote a noteworthy study on the image of Jesus in Islam,[5] finds, for example, the 'extremely theocentric theology (!) of Muḥammad which led him to deny the divinity of Jesus', extraordinarily 'egocentric'. Allegedly, Muḥammad's own experiences became the criterion he used to evaluate the past. The past should be relevant for the present. Räisänen maintains that 'the Koran's image of Jesus must also be seen in this context'.

An image of Jesus based on the study of isolated passages of the Koran must be rejected as faulty and deficient. All the particular characteristics the Koran ascribes to Jesus correspond, or are parallel, to those of this prophetic predecessors. Adam, who is also a prophet of Islam, was born in a fashion similar to Jesus (Sura, 3:59). Among other miracles, Moses called forth the dead to life.

Muḥammad, on the contrary, stands in sharp contrast to his predecessors. He personally attributed no great value to miracles. He declared the Koran to be his mightiest sign, his miracle (*muᶜjiza*), the good news of salvation spoken without preparation by an illiterate or semi-illiterate. When his young son Ibrāhīm was laid to his rest, a solar eclipse took place. The people immediately began to say that heaven mourned the offspring of God's apostle. When Muḥammad heard this interpretation, he rejected it as non-Muslim. Consequently, how can one regard the image of Jesus in the Koran as a creation of Muḥammad, on the basis of his own experiences of the actualized past? Why should Islamic theology be characterized as 'egocentric' as regards Muḥammad? What then is one to say of the theology of the Old Testament, with the people of Israel at its centre, or of the theology of the New Testament in which Jesus is the central figure?

Considering the kind of conclusions which may emerge from otherwise serious studies (for instance, those of Räisänen), it is easy to see how issues can become confused. Obviously, strong reactions have been forthcoming from the Muslim side. Today it is no different. Among Muslim scholars who have been enticed out of their reserve about the problem of Jesus is the illustrious al-Ghazzālī (d. 1111) who composed a tract against the divinity of Jesus (however, the authenticity of this work has been strongly challenged recently). All in all, a great deal of polemical literature on the issue has been composed in Arabic, Turkish, Persian and Urdu.[6]

A virtual flood of very emotional apologetic writings appeared at the turn of the century, for with the beginning of the decline of the Ottoman empire, Islam took note of the bolder attacks of missionaries. Not until the rise of national interests among the reawakened peoples of the Near East was there a discernible dampening of emotions. Both Muslims and Christians now endeavour to avoid sterile and destructive confrontations on dogmatic issues. Tolerance is strongly encouraged by leading government figures. The conflict in Palestine made tolerance an imperative in Arab lands. On the other hand, political realities have fostered certain questionable tendencies in theology. The attempt has been renewed among the Arabs to give Jesus as messiah (*al-masīḥ*) a merely historical significance. According to this point of view, Jesus did indeed come as the promised messiah of the Jews, but he failed to fufil his rôle in the expected way. In place of the longed-for Jewish national state, Jesus proclaimed the Kingdom of Heaven. With the close of his mission, all chance for the coming of a new messiah was lost. Such interpretations are offered in response to various statements about the messianic character of the State of Israel.

Whatever position one adopts in regard to the stories of the prophets, the fact remains that they play an effective rôle in the formation of the general world-view of a pious Muslim. The image of Jesus in Muslim theology—if we understand it in the broader sense of doctrine—is determined by the Koran. What was revealed to Muḥammad remains true today, for the truth of the Koran, as divinely inspired, is immutable and perennial.

The most important passages of the Koran which cast light on the figure of Jesus are offered in translation:

> He said: 'Nay, I am only a messenger from thy Lord (to announce) to thee the gift of a holy son'. She said: 'How shall I have a son, seeing that no man has touched me, and I am not unchaste?' He said: 'So (it will be): Thy Lord saith "That is easy for Me" and "(We wish) to appoint him as a sign unto men and a mercy from Us": it is a matter (so) decreed'. So she conceived him, and she retired with him to a remote place. And the pains of childbirth drove her to the trunk of a palm tree: She cried (in her anguish): 'Ah! Would that I had died before this, would that I had been a thing forgotten and out of sight!' (Sura 19:19–24).

Abū Zahra (d. 1974), one of the few Muslim Christologists, notes that the unmediated creative will of God manifested itself in the case of Jesus. He was a sign of divine presence for those who were accustomed to view the world according to the usual order of things, in which a specific cause always produces a specific result.

In Jesus, however, the effect took place without the determined cause.[7]

Further, suggests Abū Zahra, the birth of Jesus revealed the world of the Spirit for men who deny it. Other Koranic passages corroborate this position:

> And she who guarded her chastity, so We breathed into her from Our spirit, and made her and her son a sign for the nations (Sura 21: 91).

To refute the divinity of Jesus, the Koran recounts the following episode:

> And behold! Allah will say: 'O Jesus the son of Mary! Didst thou say unto men, "Worship me and my mother as gods in derogation of Allah?"' He will say: 'Glory to Thee! Never could I say what I had no right to say. Had I said such a thing, Thou wouldst indeed have known it. Thou knowest what is in my heart, though I know not what is in Thine. For Thou knowest in full all that is hidden' (Sura 5:119).

With this passage as his starting point, Muḥammad ibn al-Khaṭīb, another theologian from the circle of al-Azhar scholars, remarks polemically: 'Those who maintain that Jesus is God do not really believe it themselves'.[8] He points out that Christ repeatedly refers to himself as Son of Man.[9] Ibn al-Khaṭīb interprets the remark in the Koran that Mary and her Son ate as all other men do as a delicate way of describing the human situation, characterized as it is by the taking in of food, in which man resembles the animal. The Koran wants, accordingly, to point out the absurdity of worshipping a man.

On the basis of intensive study of Koranic passages, Riyāḍ ad-Durūbiyya comes to the conclusion that Islam recognizes Jesus neither as God nor as Son of God. He concedes to Jesus merely the mission of an Israelite messenger of salvation (apostle of God) to whom a particular book, namely the Gospel, was given.[10]

The Koranic designation for Jesus, *al-Masīḥ*, is highly contested. Owing to Jewish and Christian tradition, the term came to be understood as the 'Messiah of the last day'. Closely bound up, indeed identical with this messianic image, is the notion of the coming *Mahdī*, the saviour of the Muslim world. Among the Muslim masses, the belief still lives on that before the end of the world, Jesus (*ᶜIsā*) will appear and lead the world to Islam.[11] In the past, the idea of the Mahdī inspired many adventurers and helped them to gain power and influence over simple people. Politicians have exploited it for their own advantage, as with the Mahdī uprising in the Sudan in 1882–85. Belief in the return of Jesus, whether as saviour of Islam or in any other function, directly contradicts Muslim doctrine, as influential modern theologians have asserted. 'The Koran is the final and definitive revelation', writes Ḥusein Djozo, graduate of Al-Azhar, in the official organ of the Islamic Society of Yugoslavia.[12] 'Accordingly, there is neither need nor cause for another embassy from God.' 'Expectation of the return of Christ was accompanied by an illusion which diverted Muslims from real life. It greatly helped to make the people passive, and strengthened a fatalistic attitude toward the world. In this atmosphere, specific patterns of religious behaviour emerged, e.g. *tawakkul* (passivity in manner of life), *qisma* or *kismet* (willing submission to the fate determined by God), and so on'.[13] In his observations, Djozo relies on the competent studies of the Jesus problem of the former rector of Al-Azhar, Maḥmūd Shalṭūṭ.

I am indebted to Ḥāris Korkut, another Al-Azhar scholar living in Beirūt, who drew my attention to the fact that the designation *al-Masīḥ*, in connexion with the name *ᶜĪsā* (Jesus) in the Koran, is to be understood only as a title or an address (*ᶜunwān*). No further importance should be attached to it.

Despite the respect, therefore, which Muslims show towards Jesus as a messenger sent by God, no practical results are likely to come from Muslim–Christian dialogue in regard to Christ. In a time when biblical miracles prove less and less convincing, the Koranic image of Jesus, laden with legendary chimeras, threatens to fade even more. On the other hand, the western theologians who distance themselves from the God of revelation, open up a gulf which could make Muslim–Christian dialogue impossible. Only a return to the common source, belief in God, and common ethico-social and religious objectives can guarantee meaningful dialogue and productive co-operation.

Notes

1. See F. Buri, J. M. Lochman and H. Ott, *Dogmatik im Dialog*, Vol. 2 (Gütersloh, 1974), p. 13. It should be noted that this essay has not taken into consideration Muslim mysticism (*taṣawwuf*) and the religious ideas of popular piety, since they do not properly belong to our topic.
2. Sura 12:4.
3. The term 'covenant', which occasionally appears in the Koran in the context of the story of the origin of Islam, has a totally different meaning from the 'covenant' of the Old Testament.
4. Cf. A. Merad, *Le Christ selon le Coran* (Aix-en-Provence, 1968), p. 80. Further, Muḥammad Kāmil Ḥusain, *City of Wrong. A Friday in Jerusalem*. Transl. from the Arabic with an introduction by Kenneth Cragg (Djambatan, 1959, XXV, 225). Cf. also Elsa Sophia von Kamphoevener, *Islamische Christuslegenden* (Zürich, 1963), 53 pp.
5. H. Räisänen, *Das koranische Jesusbild. Ein Beitrag zur Theologie des Korans* (Helsinki, 1971), p. 89.
6. For the earlier period see M. Steinschneider, *Polemische und apologetische Literatur in arabischer Sprache zwischen Muslimen, Christen und Juden* (Leipzig, 1877). Cf. also the contribution by Peter Antes in the present work.
7. Muḥammad Abū Zahra, *Maḥḍarāt fi'n-naṣrāniyya* (Lectures on Christianity) (Cairo 1385, h/1965–6), pp. 16 f. Abū Zahra was professor at al-Azhar until his death in 1964.
8. Muḥammad ibn al-Khaṭīb, *Hādhā huwa'l-ḥaqq* (Cairo 1386/1966–7), p. 6. This work was composed in answer to an abusive attack on Islam from the pen of a Christian theologian.
9. *Op. cit.*, p. 11. Cf. also Riyāḍ ad-Darūbiyya (El Droubie), *A Muslim View of Jesus and Christianity* (London, n.d., c. 1975) p. 4.
10. *id.*, p. 17.
11. ᶜAbdallāh ibn ᶜUmar al-Baiḍāwī (d. 1286)—one of the most respected commentators on the Koran—was the scholar who expanded the doctrine of the return of Jesus. See Räisänen, *op. cit.*, p. 22.
12. Husein Djozo in the paragraph: 'Questions and answers' (*Pitanja i odgovori*), in: *Glasnik Vrhovnog islamskog starješinstva* 37 (Sarajevo, 1974), p. 44.
13. Djozo, *loc cit.*, p. 46.

The Image of Jesus in Contemporary Exegesis

Joseph Blank

I

In a Marian hymn the poet Novalis says:

> I see you in a thousand images,
> Mary, lovingly portrayed . . .[1]

What Novalis says about Mary the mother of Jesus, can probably be maintained today even more fittingly of Jesus, her son. Jesus also encounters us in modern exegesis, more or less 'lovingly' or 'pleasingly' and in 'a thousand images'. And we may well suppose that all these images fall short of what the believing soul perceives in him.

It is extremely difficult, if not impossible, to depict the 'image of Jesus' in contemporary Christian exegesis. I can only try to set forth briefly a few of the problems of contemporary research about Jesus. In so doing we must keep two scarcely inseparable factors in mind: the figure of the historical Jesus appears, according to the New Testament witnesses, as intimately related to the origin and formulation of the primitive Christian faith in Jesus, and therefore in the context of confession—whatever its form—that Jesus is the Messiah of God. There are very few cases where, from the start, historical tradition and interpretation of this tradition have been so tightly intermeshed and amalgamated (because of experience of faith) as in the case of Jesus of Nazareth. Perhaps the Old Testament legends of the patriarchs or the Exodus traditions afford the best analogies. In general it was the Old Testament tradition which best prepared the ground for this way of thinking. Socrates might be a parallel if rather different phenomenon. As is well-known, Jesus of Nazareth himself set nothing down in writing; this is not a discovery of modern exegesis; Christian tradition knew it from the beginning. None of the canonical gospels is traced back to Jesus as author and again no book in the apocryphal gospel literature of the second or third century AD specifically designates Jesus as an author. What is significant is that no single New Testament witness distinctly claims to be authorized by Jesus Christ uniquely and in contrast to all others. No Christian is obliged to believe in Jesus as an author; and thus to connect the gospels directly with Jesus as an author; that has always been clear, not only in modern critical theology. All the gospels are historical transmissions about Jesus, and in that sense, witnesses and result of the Jesus tradition of the primitive Church. Therefore one special problem arises when Islam sets Christians alongside Jews as 'people of a book', for a secondary characteristic has been made to seem decisive.

The 'thousand images' of Jesus did not come into existence arbitrarily. In the four canonical gospels the New Testament itself handed on four very different images of Jesus. The ancient Church sensed these differentiations when, for example, it described John's gospel as the pneumatic gospel, in contrast to the Synoptics with their greater stress on the human and historical elements. Only exegesis in its most recent phase, with the aid of redaction criticism, has taught us how vastly different the understanding of Jesus is, not only between John and the Synoptics, but among the Synoptics themselves, and that we are dealing with four different images of Jesus, and with four different interpretations of the message of Jesus: that is, of the Gospel. Whereas in Matthew Jesus is above all the unique teacher, in Mark he is the hidden Messiah, Son of God, the subduer of the demonic powers of evil. The Jesus of Luke's gospel is the saviour and benefactor of men, the friend of outcasts, who was first recognized by poor shepherds and died in fraternal solidarity with a criminal. In John he is the incarnate word of God, the bearer of eschatological revelation.

It is noteworthy that encounters with Jesus or with the Jesus tradition led to such essentially differing images of Jesus. Of course this means that it is simply impossible to construct a coherent '*vita*' or rather *historia Jesu* on the basis of the four gospels, even if it is seen only as a history of his public works. Any attempt of this kind meets with insurmountable difficulties. The Johannine conception cannot be integrated into the framework underlying Mark, and *vice versa*. Likewise the journey narrative in Luke (Lk 9:51–18:14) breaks out of the framework of Mark (Mk 9:50–10:1), which is rather modest in comparison. The same is true of the discourses in Matthew. Even details contradict one another: did Jesus' public life last three or one and a half years or even less? Did he preach often in Jerusalem, or just once before his death, in connexion with the Last Passover? Was Galilee the centre of his activity, or was it Jerusalem? Is the date of Jesus' death 15 Nisan, the Passover feast, or 14 Nisan, the preparation day for the feast? What exactly transpired at the arrest, trial and judgment of Jesus? Were there proceedings before the Sanhedrin? If yes, of what nature? What was the final upshot? Where does the primary responsibility for Jesus' death lie? and so on. If these questions have given rise to fairly heated controversy up to our day, then the cause is to be found at least partially in the Evangelists' diverse presentations.

The need to obviate these difficulties existed already in primitive Christianity. Tatian the Syrian was probably the first to attempt a harmony of the gospels, perhaps based upon an apocryphal gospel: that is, a complete, as far as possible uninterrupted, logical sequence of the *historia Jesu*.[2] The fact that this gospel harmony, the Diatessaron, was copied and translated up until the Middle Ages shows how popular Tatian's undertaking was. The effort to arrive at as unified an image of Jesus as possible springs not only from historical and literary interests, for dogmatic Christology is a continuous attempt to bring the different images of Jesus presented by the gospels into a uniform overall concept by the use of a dogmatic formula. The gospel harmony and the dogmatically uniform formula, each in its own way, represent an impoverishment of the New Testament witnesses for Jesus. Today, for the first time, we are beginning to see the variety of images of Jesus as something positive. This means that we must accept that the New Testament offers no exclusive or normative image of Jesus, but a number of very diverse images of Jesus. If we take into consideration the non-gospel material in the New Testament, including Paul, we can add even more to the total. We have to distinguish carefully between the one Jesus of Nazareth, who as a historical person was presupposed by all these images, and a tetramorphic or, more accurately, plurimorphic interpretation of Jesus. In this sense we can adopt E. Schweizer's formulation: 'Jesus is the man who confounds all schemas'.[3]

II

Given the above presuppositions, how is the quest for the historical Jesus to be evaluated? Surely it implies, as Heinrich Schlier suggests, 'a practical rejection of the canonical character of Holy Scripture, so that the reconstruction of the historical Jesus becomes a fifth gospel and the ultimate criterion of the other four'.[4] Or is the search for the historical Jesus behind the primitive Christian *kerygma* an attempt of *homo peccator* to obtain a false security, instead of remaining satisfied with simple faith?

Although we have four different images of Jesus in the gospels, it is nonetheless clear that all these images and interpretations have one common point of reference, one central point, so that they all refer to a single figure, the person of Jesus. They all wish to depict the one Jesus, and not a series of different Jesuses. Hence the insoluble tension between the one Jesus and diverse interpretations of Jesus is part of the New Testament as we have it. We also find in the four gospels a series of parallel sayings which offer elements of a *historia Jesu*. The most important of these is the account of the execution of Jesus on the cross by a regiment under the command of the Roman procurator, Pontius Pilatus. The connexion between the movement inspired by Jesus and the baptismal movement centring on John the Baptist is testified to by diverse and independent traditions, a fact that is the more important since, apparently, conflict and competition between these groups were confusing the issue. Here I cannot enumerate all such convergences, of which there is a substantial number.

Finally, form criticism and redaction criticism have provided us with an excellent method of investigating what lies behind given texts: that is, of discovering the supposedly most primitive beginnings of a tradition underlying the texts we have in their final written form in the gospels. Such an investigation according to the critical methodology of modern scholarship is far removed from mere subjective caprice. The various methodological steps of the historical investigation, beginning with a comparison of the Synoptics, can be clearly traced and scientifically established. Today those who maintain the total historical validity of the gospels more or less indiscriminately, rather than offer serious source criticism on the basis of the two-source theory, as well as form-tradition and redaction criticism, seem to arrive at conclusions about the *historia Jesu* that are far less certain than those formulated by critical exegesis, which are carried out at a relatively high reflective level of scholarly methodology.

C. Lachmann, C. H. Weisse, and C. J. Wilke worked out the classic form of the two-source theory a hundred and forty years ago. According to this theory, Mark is the oldest written gospel and the source for Matthew and Luke (the 'principle of Mark on priority'). In addition to Mark, Matthew and Luke are also said to have made use of a collection of dominical sayings, the so-called logia source Q. 'One proof offered for the existence of this source Q is the extensive literal agreement between Matthew and Luke in the material common to them that does not stem from Mark'.[5] It is not clear whether Q represents a literary source or a 'level of tradition . . . which stands considerably nearer to the oral parenetic and literal tradition and was subject to the process of change to a greater extent than Mark'.[6] The most recent studies of Q[7] include the hypothesis of a written source which in contrast to Mark, was lost. The two-source theory has in fact established itself as the most convincing and fruitful solution to the synoptic problem. Markan priority, however (priority in a literary sense and primarily signifying nothing more than Mark's literary priority over Matthew and Luke), may not be used uncritically to answer historical questions, for on the level of tradition-criticism one often has the impression that, over against the Q tradition, Mark may well be secondary. Furthermore, it is undeniable that there are many cross-connexions between the Q tradition and the Markan tradition.

Even the Q tradition, however, fails to provide us with direct conclusions about the 'historical Jesus'. Even in this tradition, we must reckon with the further development and interpretation of the oldest Jesus tradition. According to Siegfried Schulz, the most primitive level of tradition in Q is determined by the following factors:

1. a post-Easter prophetic enthusiasm;
2. apocalyptic expectation of the imminent second coming;
3. charismatic refinement of the Torah;
4. Son-of-Man Christology

Serious critical objections may be brought against Schulz's position. Schulz offers an *a priori* connexion of the oldest level of tradition with the prophetic and enthusiastic formation of the community, without investigating the historical Jesus. For Schulz, any feed-back to the historical Jesus is subsequent and secondary. He says 'The quest for the historical Jesus in no way stands at the beginning of primitive Christianity and its proclamation'.[8] Here he unilaterally adopts Ernst Käsemann's view that the post-Easter primitive community was the first to think in an apocalyptic framework. What is involved here is, in my opinion, a problematic *a priori* insistence on a 'non-apocalyptic Jesus'. According to this widely-accepted position, Jesus's mission may be characterized as 'eschatological', but not as 'apocalyptic'. Apocalyptic enthusiasm at first took hold only of the post-Easter community. Paul Hoffmann in his *Studien zur Logienquelle* adopts a different position which seems to me to be historically more plausible and more coherent. He lays stress on the objective continuity between the preaching of Jesus and the *logia* source, which in his view seems to be grounded exactly in the apocalyptic character of Jesus's proclamation. As for the problem of 'imminent eschatological expectation' P. Hoffmann says: 'Q takes over Jesus' sayings in which he speaks of the breaking in of the *basileia* by means of his works and adopts them to its own situation, without, however, weakening them'[9]. According to Hoffmann, then, in Q the proclamation of Jesus is interpreted from its own post-Easter situation. Both Hoffmann and Schulz posit a group or community as transmitters of the Q tradition. Hoffmann puts forth the interesting thesis that the Q-group consisted of a group of Jewish–Christian disciples of Jesus who proclaimed the message of Jesus as repentance and peace during the time of interior fermentation before the beginning of the Jewish war.

Form criticism, furthermore, has taught us to take every piece of tradition, every pericope, every individual logion individually, and to examine it carefully from all aspects. This method, however, seems at the present to be leading to a cul-de-sac. Recently, Stock rightly cautioned us to remember that the inquiries into the history of tradition (particularly those into ideas and motifs) are often independent of the individual text and its interpretation.[10] When, as is usual today, exegeses of a single pericope extend to three hundred pages, then something is wrong.

III

This leads us to a second consideration. It is necessary for New Testament criticism to move away from a purely immanent consideration of New Testament texts and to make more use of Jewish secular and religious history to illuminate the New Testament texts. This seems to be a future area for intensive study.

The orientation of dialectical theology to biblical theology caused extensive neglect of historical questions in Old Testament and New Testament studies. The result has certainly been a certain narrowing of perspective. If not only the figure of Jesus, his words and deeds, but the rise of primitive Christianity and its consequences are to be understood historically, they must be seen first within the context of Judaism, and more precisely, Judaism under Roman domination, in the period after the destruction of the second temple. In this connexion it is evident that the discovery of the Qumran library provided an unexpected advance in our knowledge of early Judaism, and that it has given and will continue to give an enormous impetus to scholarship, offering interpreters material for new questions on the whole of early Jewish literature, especially apocalyptic.[11] The 'apocalyptic period' of Judaism, from 167 BC to AD 135 is of profound significance for an understanding of Judaism and primitive Christianity. It is an advantage to all sides, that today the early Jewish literature is no longer investigated merely for the sake of and in connexion with the New Testament, and that in place of the term 'late Judaism' 'early Judaism' has been adopted to designate this era; this fits the historical data.

In rough outline, the following factors seem important. First, we now know that early Judaism before the destruction of the second temple was neither closed nor homogeneous, but a complex of various competing groups and religious parties, each with its own distinctive theological position. The 'true Israel' is, therefore, a matter of dispute. Against this background, the movements of John the Baptist and Jesus appear at first sight just two groups within a broad framework of diverse Jewish groups. The close ties between the baptismal movement of John the Baptist and Jesus' own movement are repeatedly emphasized in the New Testament and are decisive for a more precise historical differentiation. Any other direct positive connexion with or influence from other tendencies within Judaism, such as the Essenes, Pharisees, Sadducees, Zealots, cannot be clearly proven. If there was any tie between Jesus and Qumran, then it was through the mediation of John the Baptist. Most New Testament scholars, however, are now rather sceptical of such a link. Given the rival notions in early Judaism of piety, true worship and even the question of Torah practice (the Pharisees accepted the oral Torah while the Sadducees rejected it), an objective historical inquiry, provided it has no *a priori* dogmatic or apologetic presuppositions, must first try to comprehend these various conceptions and describe them as accurately as possible. The proclamations of Jesus also have to be situated in this many-faceted world of early Judaic ideas. This comparison should reveal what is specific to Jesus' message. What specifically characterizes Jesus's own message, in my opinion, is first his concrete expectation of the imminent eschatological reign of God: 'The time is fulfilled, and the kingdom of God is at hand!' (Mk 1:15) or, as Bultmann puts it: 'What is new and his own is the certitude with which he says "Now the time has come! The reign of God has begun. The end is here!"'[12]

It seems somewhat futile always to ask: What is Jewish and what is original to Jesus in his preaching? The entire message of Jesus has Jewish roots and influences; that is beyond doubt. It should however be plain that Jesus accepted the Jewish traditions of faith and life in his own independent way, and that he transformed them so as to form an original, all-embracing eschatological concept. There is a connexion with the book of Isaiah, especially Deutero- and Trito-Isaiah, though of course Jesus' age did not possess our knowledge of the scientific divisions within Isaiah. The historical Jesus is through and through a Palestinian-Jewish figure from early Judaism. By no means, however, can he simply he depicted as an ordinary orthodox pious Jew. He rejected, for example, the binding power of the oral Halakha, yet was not a Sadducee. It also seems clear that Jesus cannot be counted among any of the four known religious parties. He has least in common with the Sadducees, the party of the priestly nobility, the temple aristocracy and the notables. In his recent work, *Jesus und die Sadduzäer*, Karlheinz Müller convincingly demonstrates that the real opponents of Jesus were not the pious Pharisees, but the party of the Sadducean priestly aristocracy.[13] Müller reaches the conclusion: 'The Sadducees categorically denied the Pharisean Halakha, and by doing so, every enactment of an ethical Torah interpretation[14] which tried to reach an accommodation to the actual human situation. They therefore dispensed themselves from the responsibility of newly integrating the law into the changing conditions of society. Their interest lay in preserving the *status quo* . . .

The preaching and activity of Jesus of Nazareth had to end in incessant confrontation with their ideology of total immanence ... Here an eschatological message in the strict sense of the word, which uncompromisingly respected the prerogatives of God in regard to his definitive reign, which was expected to occur in the immediate future, encountered head on the conservativism of ancient Jewish orthodoxy'.[15] Other people also collided with the class of the theocratic leaders, the Sadducees, in the time immediately before the Jewish war, as we know from the reports of Flavius Josephus. Herod's execution of John the Baptist should be mentioned in this context though John the Baptist was no political figure. If the Pharisees appear to be the real opponents of Jesus in the New Testament texts, especially in Matthew, that is because they alone survived as a group the destruction of the second temple and hence were the very group with whom early Christianity had to contend after AD 70. Matthew and Luke were indeed composed after the year AD 70. The later confrontation between the Christian community and Judaism as now dominated by Phariseeism, was projected back into the time of Jesus. This is not to say that there could not have been any confrontations at all between Jesus and the Pharisees. Surely some existed, but hardly of such profound importance. The New Testament witnesses agree that in the tradition of the passion narratives, the Pharisees do not appear as participants. That may be historically correct. Continued investigation in this direction promises a deeper understanding of the message of Jesus and of all the factors which finally led to the formation of Christianity, and to a removal of the many prejudices which still exist between Christians and Jews. In this context, we must mention that only quite recently have Jewish scholars taken part in the quest for Jesus. Pinchas G. Lapide observes that 'more books about Jesus by Jewish authors have appeared in the last twenty-five years than in the preceding nineteen centuries'. Lapide himself recently published a work which makes an important contribution to the discussion.[16] I personally expect a great deal from this new development, for there are many aspects of the historical Jesus which Jews can probably understand better than Christians.

Nevertheless, we must continually pose the question: Why did Jesus have precisely the effect he did and why did the Jewish Jesus-sect eventually become the world religion we know as Christianity?

IV

What does the *historia Jesu* look like today according to the approximate consensus of critical scholarship?

In all likelihood, Jesus of Nazareth was born 'during the days of Herod' (Mt 2:1; Lk 1:5). His home and probably his place of birth was Nazareth in Galilee, apparently a locality of no importance in the time of Jesus. Since Herod the Great died in 4 BC, the generally suggested date for the birth of Jesus is 6 or 7 BC. Mt. 2:1 and Lk 2:4 place Jesus' birth in Bethlehem, the city of David, but this is on the basis of the particular literary and theological aspects of the story of Jesus' childhood in Matthew and Luke, and is therefore doubted by critical scholars. The infancy narratives, relating late developments from the point of view of tradition history, may be regarded as historical sources only with the greatest caution. We know nothing about the childhood and youth of Jesus.

Jesus first becomes a historically tangible force in connexion with the appearance of John the Baptist, which Luke sets out with more or less accurate chronology (Lk 3:18). The fifteenth year of the reign of Tiberius is usually reckoned from the beginning of his absolute sovereignty, therefore from AD 14. This is not certain, however. It could also mean the beginning of his co-regency with Augustus in AD 11. So we calculate that John the Baptist's activities began in AD 26–28. We cannot clearly ascertain how long John was active; even the exact date of his death is unknown. What is certain, however, is that (as both the New Testament—Mk 6:17; Mt 14:3–12—and Flavius Josephus 18/118, report) John was executed at the order of Herod Antipas and that this took place before Jesus' crucifixion. This is not sufficiently taken into account in the literature about Jesus, although it could be exceedingly enlightening in regard to Jesus.

At first, Jesus attached himself to John's movement and approved of his ministry in every respect.[17] The baptism of Jesus by John is sufficiently well-founded (Mk 1:9–11 par) to be taken as historical, for the primitive Church regarded it as a singularly unacceptable matter. After his baptism, perhaps Jesus separated himself from John's movement. According to Mk 1:14 (par. Mt 4:12; Lk 3:19) Jesus began his own ministry directly after the arrest of John. According to John (Jn 1:35 ff; 3:22–40; 4:1 f.) Jesus's ministry was contemporaneous for a period with John's. This seems less plausible to me. 'Jesus probably began his own ministry AD 28, in any case not later than AD 29. How long did his public ministry last? . . . Most likely . . . a little over two years, and if we date the crucifixion in the year 30, the beginning of his ministry would be between AD 28 and 30'.[18]

Jesus appeared as an eschatological prophet, as a messenger of God's imminent reign. In my opinion one must see and understand his entire ministry from this fundamental perspective. Jesus directed his eschatological message of the reign of God to the Jews of his time and, indeed, to Judaism in its totality. Not the various messianic pretenders of the Jewish liberation movement, the Zealots, but rather the great Old Testament prophets and their actions are the prototypes of the figure of Jesus and his ministry. Clearly Jesus shared in the apocalyptic expectation; he is convinced of the imminent coming of God's reign, and it is this expectation which alone explains his ministry, particularly his life as a wandering preacher who roams through the country from one place to the other. The journey to Jerusalem also belongs totally to this picture: there Jesus had to seek the *crisis*. As a wandering preacher he collected disciples, companions, and followers, whom he made familiar with his message and (this is a particular feature) whom he bound to his own person; the disciples should 'follow' Jesus as their master. The selection of the Twelve (which I consider to be historical) fits admirably into the concept of the message of the eschatological reign. For Jesus was concerned to gather and restore the 'true Israel', the people of God with its eschatological integrity, as was promised for the end-time. Because he was pressured by time, Jesus gave his disciples a share in his task of proclamation.

Like the prophecies of Deutero-Isaiah, the proclamation of Jesus is essentially the good news of salvation, *evangelion*, even though Jesus did not use the term. God's salvation is to be available to all, especially to sinners. Jesus used unusual methods to draw the 'tax collectors and sinners' back into the community of God, and these methods apparently shocked and scandalized pious Jews. To these methods belongs the meal, with its eschatological sign-value. The significance of the meal for Jesus must be seen in the context of his radical message of God's eschatological reign, since the meal is so to speak an anticipation of the coming final salvation. Jesus's radical interpretation of the Torah, with the supreme command to love one's enemies, also belongs together with this message of God's reign; its motivation is eschatological. The Pharisees were interested in humanizing obedience to the Torah; in making it practicable for everyday life; but Jesus goes still a step farther and makes God's will practicable for the *am-haaretz*, which means that the study of the Torah is basically superfluous. This is indeed eschatological radicalism, and here Jesus was close to all radical enthusiasts. Finally eschatology offers the key to understanding the symbolic action of purifying the temple. Jesus was obviously convinced of the end of the temple and its cult. The strange temple logion: 'This man said, I will destroy this temple made by hands, and in three days build up another, not made by hands' (Mk 14:57; par. Mt 26:61 f; Jn 2:19) is, in my opinion, a genuine saying of Jesus, and fits his apocalyptic thinking. The temple which should take the place of the earthly temple is the eschatological temple. Exactly for this reason he attracts the animosity of the temple aristocracy. In any case, one must make use of eschatological and/or apocalyptic as a key for fully understanding Jesus.

Jesus unquestionably saw his own mission as centrally important to the coming of God's reign. His words and deeds are fiery signs of God's imminent reign, and he himself, in person, is the most important sign. Any closer determination of Jesus's self-consciousness is highly problematic. Certainly Jesus himself laid no claim to the title Messiah; it is always others that use it of him.

He probably spoke of the apocalyptic Son of Man. A possible self-understanding of Jesus as 'Son of God' is connected with his conviction of God's gracious Fatherhood. On Jesus' lips, it is surely not meant in any Hellenistic, numinous sense. Post-Easter Christology filled this title with still other implications. It is noteworthy that Jesus regarded his message and his works as the proof of his legitimacy and authority:

> If it is by the finger of God that I cast out demons, then the kingdom of God has come upon you (Lk 11:20)

The execution of Jesus was accomplished on the cross, in the final instance, therefore, by the Roman occupation force and its representative, the procurator, Pontius Pilatus. The execution was probably the result of the Sadducean priestly aristocracy, who at that time also were the majority in the Sanhedrin, and the Roman procurator acting in unison. Karlheinz Müller, in the article already mentioned, points out an extremely interesting parallel to the trial of Jesus in Flavius Josephus.[19] Flavius Josephus relates an incident about a man named Jesus, son of Ananias, 'an uneducated rustic', who in the year 62 at the feast of the Tabernacles, appeared in Jerusalem as a prophet of doom and prophesied the destruction of the city. Among other things, the text says:

> Some of the leading citizens, incensed at these ill-omened words, arrested the fellow and severally chastised him. But he without a word on his own behalf or for the private ear of those who smote him, only continued his cries as before. Thereupon, the magistrates supposing, as was indeed the case, that the man was under some supernatural impulse, brought him before the Roman governor; there, although flayed to the bone with scourges, he neither sued for mercy nor shed a tear, but merely introduced the most mournful of variations into his ejaculation, responding to each stroke with 'Woe to Jerusalem!' When Albinus, the governor, asked him who and whence he was and why he uttered these cries, he answered never a word, but unceasingly reiterated his dirge

over the city, until Albinus pronounced him a maniac and let him go.

The parallels are so convincing that one cannot easily ignore them. According to K. H. Müller, 'we are dealing here with an apparently firmly established successive appeal process: the Sadducean nobility take the prophet of doom by force, interrogate him while beating him, and finally hand him over to the procurator who has him scourged and who at the same time conducts an official interrogation'.[20] That a popular movement of an avowedly religious nature can be regarded as politically dangerous is aptly illustrated by the case of John the Baptist. One need not, therefore, argue *a posteriori* in Jesus' case to political ambition after the style of the Zealots. The accusation against Jesus, that he claimed to be the king of the Jews, may express the Romans' understanding of Jesus as a Zealot leader; a plausible cause for execution was needed. This was actually found in the public ministry of Jesus, which did bring unrest. It would be a short step to explain such unrest as politically explosive, and then seize upon a juridically effective notion: *basileus tōn Ioudaion*. Jesus died as a rebel against the Roman state, though he had probably never been interested in it as such.

V

As for the formation of the post-Easter community, the primitive Church, the formation of the Jewish sect of the Nazoreans, those who confess Jesus as Messiah, I maintain the traditional view that this new association of Jesus' disciples after his horrible execution on the cross is not conceivable without the whole complex of the Easter event, the 'raising of Jesus from the dead'. However, I do not want to disentangle the details of this complex. From a historical perspective it means that the real historical impact of Jesus began only after his death. One must contend with, and explain this fact, or not grasp the essential nature of Christianity. I feel that one cannot understand the essence of Christianity without seriously dealing with the fact of religious history. The primitive community regards Jesus as a living power, fulfilling and authoritatively determining them. They see in him the Messiah, but give this title a completely new meaning. They describe him as 'Son of Man' and await his return in glory. At the same time the community decisively follows the Crucified. Henceforth, for the followers of Jesus belief in God is irrevocably connected with Jesus's revelation of God, with Jesus's way of perceiving God, and with his interpretation of God's will. At the same time, primitive Christianity maintains lasting ties derived from the God of Israel. Paul calls Jesus 'the image of God' (2 Kor. 4:5). Here, it is decisive that the post-Easter followers of Jesus, the *Christianoi*, as outsiders soon named them (Acts 11:26; 26:28; 1 Pet. 4:16), from the very beginning tried to offer an interpretation of the message of Jesus that was also an enactment of it. It is clear from the diverse images of Jesus that in a certain sense, Christianity is a 'world religion *malgré soi'*. Any triumphalist attempt by ecclesiastical leaders to invoke Jesus as a figure to legitimate their rule is constantly thwarted by the crucified Jesus, who challenges men to follow him.

Notes

1. Cf. Novalis, *Die Dichtungen,* E. Wasmuth (Heidelberg, 1953), p. 436.
2. C. AD 170; cf. BHHW, III 1933. For the diatessaron cf. *id.* I, p. 455 f.
3. E. Schweizer, *Jesus* (London & Richmond, 1971). p. 23.
4. Cf. H. Schlier, *Das Ende der Zeit* (Freiburg i.Br., 1971), p. 11.
5. Wikenhauser-Schmid, *Introduction*, p. 280.
6. G. Bornkamm in *Die Religion in Geschichte und Gegenwart*, 3rd. ed., II, p. 756.
7. D. Lührmann, *Die Redaktion der Logienquelle* (Neukirchen, 1969); P. Hoffmann, *Studien zur Theologie der Logienquelle* (Münster i.W., 1972), and S. Schulz, *Q—Die Spruchquelle der Evangelisten* (Zürich, 1972).
8. S. Schulz, *op. cit.,* p. 482.
9. P. Hoffmann, *op. cit*., p. 37.
10. Cf. A. Stock, *Umgang mit theologischen Texten* (1974) p. 25.
11. See particularly the compilation edited by J. Maier & J. Schreiner, *Literatur und Religion des Frühjudentums* (Würzburg, 1973).
12. R. Bultmann, *Theologie des Neuen Testaments* (Tübigen, 1st ed. 1953), pp. 4 f.

13. Cf. Karlheinz Müller, 'Jesus und die Sadduzäer', in: *Biblische Randbemerkungen, Schülerfestschrift für Rudolf Schnackenberg, zum 60. Geburtstag*, ed. H. Merklein & J. Lange (Würzburg, 1974), pp, 3–24.
14. Flavius Josephus, *Antiquitates* 13, pp. 297–8.
15. Karlheinz Müller, *op. cit.*, pp. 21–3
16. P. E. Lapide, *Der Rabbi von Nazaret. Wandlungen des jüdischen Jesusbildes* (Trier, 1974).
17. Cf. Mt 11:2–19, par; Lk 7:23–35; 16:16;—Mk. 11:27–33, par.; Mt 21:23–27; Lk 20:1–8.
18. F. V. Filson, *A New Testament History* (Philadelphia & London, 1964).
19. Flavius Josephus, *Bellum judaicum*, VI pp. 300–5 (transl. H. St J. Thackery, Cambridge, Mass. 1928).
20. Karlheinz Müller, *op. cit.*, p. 17.

Revelation and Tradition in Islam

Rudi Paret

In Islam, one distinguishes between the Koran, which encompasses all the texts which Muhammad proclaimed as revelation, and *Ḥadīth*, the tradition which supplements or interprets the Koran. The term 'ḥadīth' is used of individual traditions and of the traditions as a whole. Among the Sunni, six extensive *ḥadīth* collections have attained canonical standing. They date from the second half of the ninth century and the beginning of the tenth century, but the individual traditions preserved within them can be traced back along a line of authorities, the so-called *Isnād*, to the time of the rise of Islam, and to a great extent, even to Muhammad himself. The Shiʿa possess similar *ḥadīth* collections.

In the relationship between the Koran and *ḥadīth*, the highest position belongs to the Koran, as the sacred scripture of Islam. Every word of the Koran is regarded as inspired; it is an inimitable linguistic miracle. Koranic texts are the essential component of liturgical prayer. The Koran serves as a source of edification for Muslims. Reciting the whole of the Koran is a pious task. The Koran is, however, neither a text-book of Muslim dogmatic theology nor a codex of Muslim jurisprudence, but a source-book for theology and jurisprudence. The *ḥadīth* also has this function. Above all, *ḥadīth* supplements the Koran in legal materials, which are less abundant in the Koran. The contents of *ḥadīth* are open to question, for not every word is inspired, and it has been transmitted by a chain of authorities. As a final court of appeal, the so-called *Ijmāᶜ*, the consensus of the Muslim community and of authorized theologians and jurists, guarantees the contents of the Koran and its text as well as the *ḥadīth.* An opinion which is commonly accepted in the community or among theologians and jurists is binding, in accordance with the traditional saying of Muhammad: 'My community will never agree to an error.'

In the second and third centuries of the Islamic era, Muslim theologians and jurists dealt extensively with the Koran and the *ḥadīth* and, especially in the area of law, developed a system of norms and regulations which governed every detail of a Muslim's public and private life. A system of law had been completed by around AD 900, at least among the Sunni. The 'door of the *ijtihād*,' the independent discernment of law, was closed. The following generations had to content themselves with what the earlier authorities had worked out, and could only make secondary inferences. As time went on, the consolidation of laws became stultified, and stagnated.

In Islam, at least in its Sunni expression, there is no organized hierarchy, no leadership rôle corresponding to the papacy, and no synods or councils. Muhammad alone, as messenger of God, had authority in the spiritual area at his disposal. Scholars who give consideration to the proper reading and interpretation of the Koran and evaluate the *ḥadīth* out of interest in dogmatic theology and juridical norms, do so not by virtue of any office but as private persons, with the weight of their reputations. This applies to the community as a whole, and to individual schools of theology and law. What a theologian or jurist maintains as his opinion has no binding authority until it is recognized by consensus.

But how can Muslims do justice to the demands of today's modern, enlightened, internationally-oriented world when they are bound to doctrines, legal norms and political objectives which their forbears accepted in the vastly different circumstances of the Middle Ages and which have not been admitted to critical scrutiny during the last thousand years? In other words, is Islam as a system of religious doctrines and of law immutable in every detail? Closer examination reveals that Islamic law, particularly civil law, has undergone and is continuing to undergo significant change. It remains questionable, however, whether Muslim theologians and jurists have accepted the new state of affairs only under duress, or whether precisely as theologians and jurists, they have appropriated the changes spiritually and can genuinely affirm them. One must reckon with the fact that principles and norms grounded in the text of the Koran or in some sense sanctioned by it can be altered much less easily than those added only after the death of Muhammad and which were committed to writing only in the *ḥadīth*. I shall now cite some examples.

The circumstances of the Caliphate question are simple. Muhammad had not foreseen the institution of the Caliphate. Accordingly, the text of the Koran provides no sanction for it. The stipulations about it in Muslim law were deduced at a later date on the basis of what had already transpired under the first four Caliphs, the so-called orthodox Caliphs. In the later Abbasid era, the Caliphate increasingly lost its original significance. After the Mongol conquest of Bagdad in 1258, the last Abbasid Caliphs lived out shadowy existences in Egypt. Later the Ottoman sultans bore the title 'Caliph'. In spring 1924 the Turkish National Assembly abolished the office of Caliph. A congress met in Cairo in 1926 to consider the Caliphate and decided that the venerable institution was no longer feasible under present circumstances. It had, so to speak, died from senility.

The obligation to wage holy war is more problematic. The Koran itself obliges Muslims 'to struggle' on God's way (*jihād*), and to stand up for the true faith with the force of arms. Specific legal prescriptions concerning *jihād*, however, were first drawn up after the onset of the great Arabic-Islamic conquests. Areas which were not, or not yet, under Arab control were regarded as war areas or, more precisely, as areas against which war had to be waged. As time passed, the demands became more modest. The conquests came to a standstill, and defeats were suffered. Today, no Muslim seriously entertains the idea of waging war against the followers of other religions. Only the most crazed fanatics still use the word *jihād* once in a while.

Legal prescriptions are most difficult to change when they are laid down in detail in the Koran, as is the case, for instance, in family matters. Let us examine more carefully what the Koran has to say about the place of women. The Koran frequently admonishes men to deal with women justly and fairly. The presuppositions dictate, however, that women are subject to men (Sura 4:34; 2:228) and have fewer rights than men. Daughters inherit only half as much as their brothers (4:11). A man's testimony equals that of two women. If a wife resists her husband, he may beat her, whereas in the reverse situation, she has to be satisfied if they both agree upon a (financial) settlement (4:24, 128). Polygamy is only of the polygynous sort (4:3—Muslims generally deduced from this verse that a man may have up to four wives at the same time). A man may 'dismiss' his wife at will and take her back again. Remarriage after a third dismissal is impossible unless the wife has married another man in the meantime and is in turn dismissed by him (2:229 f.; compare 2:231–3; 65, lv.). The dismissal of a husband by his wife is not provided for. For decades now, in various Muslim countries and at various times, legal stipulations have been introduced which aim at the reform of family law. By and large, such reform is concerned with remedying marked abuses which are not directly dependent upon Koranic formulations and which were introduced by later legal practice (for example, child marriage, the triple pronouncement of the dismissal formula, and the consequent definitive divorce by a man in a state of inebriation, and the like). Only in a few instances did the reforms touch upon the substance of Koranic law, as, for example, in the Turkish adoption of Swiss civil law in 1926 and Tunisia's prohibition of polygamy on 4 July 1958. I cannot go into detail concerning the contents of ever-advancing codifications of Muslim family law. I limit myself to a few principles or methods of argumentation in which changes directed to reform can or could be grounded. First, the door of *ijtihād*, the free productive study of law, need not remain definitively closed. In the course of the centuries, individual

Muslim theologians and jurists again and again laid claim to the right of *ijtihād*. Why should this claim not be made again today?

*Ijmā*ᶜ, the consensus of the Muslim community, could serve as a basis for the change of a given situation. *Ijmā*ᶜ, however, always lags behind. It can subsequently approve a change which has already been generally put into effect. It is not, however, apt to open doors to new forms and attitudes. The principle of compulsion (*Ḍarūra*) may be useful in attempts to justify abandoning the choice of a Caliph and participation in holy war. However, at best, it provides a basis for pardon for sins of omission, committed under pressure and at limited times, without offering any feasible grounding for a positive change and reorganization of the legal system. *Ikhtiyār* is the free choice of authorities from different legal schools, a method of argumentation which has been used now and again in the codification of family law. Authorities, however, remain authorities, whether they belong to one's own or to another school of jurisprudence, and they still stand in the way of developing legal norms by free individual choice.

Istiṣlāḥ is the final method of argumentation to be considered. It derives from *Maṣlaḥa*, roughly translated as '(common) weal', or 'public interest'. *Istiṣlāḥ*'s methods of argumentation proceed from the presupposition that in all that God has established as norms for behaviour his intention has been for *Maṣlaḥa*, the welfare of men. Therefore legal deductions which do not correspond to the idea of *Maṣlaḥa*, for instance, in the particular of family law, should be corrected accordingly. Ṭaufī, a ḥanbalite legal scholar who died in 1316, insisted radically on the method of *Istiṣlāḥ*. He, however, remained alone. The principle of *Istiṣlāḥ* has been used only sporadically, and chiefly by representatives of the malikite school of legal theory. Today this principle is once again under discussion, even in Shiᶜah circles.

This short survey of the possible means of once again setting in motion the free formation of opinion (*ijithād*), of adapting attitudes and prescriptions more than a thousand years old to contemporary conditions is confusing. Even when one applies these to practical examples and to gather illustrative material, they are not very enlightening. I do not wish to interfere in the process of renewal within the world of Islam nor to offer suggestions for a better means of modernization. The developmental process must proceed at the Muslims' own initiative. But as outsiders we may form opinions. This brings me back to my theme: revelation and tradition in Islam and their relation to one another. I am merely presenting a personal opinion. I may be biased or partial, either because I am not sufficiently well-informed, or because my viewpoint is erroneous. If that is the case, I should be corrected.

In my opinion, the representatives of Muslim theology, among whom I include representatives of traditional Muslim jurisprudence, will not do justice to the demands of the contemporary era if they limit themselves to applying Koranic formulations and later traditional material to various cases on the basis of traditional methods of interpretation. This remains a patchwork effort, regardless of the acumen and sagacity of its agents, who should instead arrive at a fundamentally new orientation. By means of a careful historical examination of the rise and development of Islam, they should perceive that much that Muḥammad and his era accepted as evident was conditioned by time and circumstances, and therefore should not be reckoned as substantive in Islam. To use a well-known term, Islam is as much in need as Christianity of demythologization. Muslim theologians have the responsibility to respond to this challenge, and must be prepared to give up accretions conditioned by time and circumstance, in order to be able to represent and defend what is essential in Muḥammad's proclamation.

From olden times, Muslim scholars have critically evaluated *ḥadīth*. They were mainly interested in scrutinizing the Isnād, the chain of authorities who were witnesses for the *ḥadīth* and regarded the texts of the tradition as genuine sayings from the time of the Prohpet, if the chain remained unbroken and was made up of trustworthy authorities. Actually, most of the texts are of later provenance and can serve as sources for facts only from the end of the seventh or first half of the eighth century. Let us take an example from Muslim law which cannot be derived from the Koran but which was conceived of only after the death of Muḥammad: the designation of *Dār al-ḥarb*, a 'war area', for the territory outside Muslim control and the obligation to *jihād*, 'holy war'. Muslim theologians must recognize that notions such as *Dār al-ḥarb* and *jihād* reflect the spirit of the age of the great Arabic wars of conquest and of the Crusades; that these notions have now outlived their usefulness and are totally anachronistic. They should no longer resort to *ḍarūra*, the pressure situation releasing one from the obligation of a law, to absolve themselves for the fact that they no longer wage holy war.

The demand for demythologization extends even to Koranic texts which, then, are proven to be authentic sayings of the Arabian Prophet. Indeed, it must extend to the whole of the Koran, not merely to isolated texts. The doctrine of literal inspiration and of *iᶜjāz*, the linguistic miracle of the Koran, is to be questioned and even more the doctrine that the Koran's very wording reaches back into eternity. In evaluating the Koran's treatment of biblical material, one must contend with the fact that Muḥammad must have become acquainted with the details of Jewish and Christian salvation history from Jewish or Christian informants and must first have assimilated it himself before he could proclaim it anew as part of his own prophetic message. If this presupposition is accepted, then contested Koranic passages become somewhat more comprehensible: for instance, the assertion that the Jews did not crucify or kill Jesus but someone resembling him (4:157) or the assertion that in days of old Abraham and Ismail constructed the Kaᶜba in Mecca (2:127).

I do not find it easy to discuss such a radically new orientation for Muslim theology. I could readily be misunderstood, particularly by Muslims who, to begin with, harbour certain suspicions of Orientalists who devote themselves to study of the Koran. Therefore, I repeat, it is not my intent to interfere with the process of renewal which is under way in the world of Islam nor to present suggestions, nor to demand more effective modernization. As an outsider, I have formulated a judgment about the present situation and I have discussed it within specialist circles. In her dissertation for the University of Tübingen, 'Revelation and History in Modern Muslim Thought', Rotraud Wielandt made a statement in this context with which I want to finish my presentation:

> One cannot avoid all misunderstandings. Nonetheless, in their study of the Koran, Islamicists must absolutely avoid everything which could give rise to the suspicion that they operate out of an intention to destroy the foundations of Muslim belief, or out of political motives, or for the sake of misconstrued enlightenment, or for the sake of Christian missionary activity, or any other such motive. The more unequivocally scholars behave in this regard, the more easily will Muslims be able to free themselves from the fear that an historical understanding of the Koran would mean the end of their religion. Instead, it could rather mean a new beginning.

The Prophet Muḥammad as a Centre of Muslim Life and Thought

Annemarie Schimmel

> Muslims will allow attacks on Allah: there are atheists and atheistic publications, and rationalistic societies; but to disparage Muḥammad will provoke from even the most 'liberal' sections of the community a fanaticism of blazing vehemence.

Wilfred Cantwell Smith wrote this in 1946 in *Islam in Modern India.*[1] Twenty years later I asked some people in a village of East Bengal (now Bangla Desh) how old some of the saints' tombs in the area might be. The headman, full of awe and veneration, answered: 'Very very old, mem, many thousand years old, like our holy Prophet . . .'

How are we to reconcile these two statements? Or, to put it in a more general way: how is the personality of Muḥammad the Prophet of Islam reflected in the life and thought of a Muslim, particularly a modern Muslim? No doubt western students of Islam have never properly understood, let alone stressed, the importance of the Prophet for a Muslim's religious life, and, as Arthur Jeffery remarks,

> . . . many years ago . . . the late Shaikh Muṣṭafā al-Marāghī remarked on a visit to his friend the Anglican bishop of Egypt, that the commonest cause of offence, generally unwitting offence, given by Christians to Muslims, arose from their

> complete failure to understand the very high regard all Muslims have for the person of their Prophet.[2]

This statement is no doubt correct. Even highly-educated people brought up in the Christian tradition find it difficult to rid themselves of ideas put about during the many centuries after the appearance of Islam had appeared on the scene. They were used to seeing in Muḥammad a seducer, a sensualist, a cunning politician, a pseudo-prophet or, at best, the founder of a Christian heresy. The scholarly studies of orientalists from the first half of the nineteenth century onward, even though still tinged by the religious or political stance of their authors, have certainly helped to contribute to a more appropriate interpretation of the Prophet and his work. Nevertheless, the faithful are suspicious of even the most recent and most objective biographies of Muḥammad written by non-Muslims. One reason for the misunderstanding of Muḥammad's personality by Westerners is his life 'in the world'. The twofold activity of the Prophet, who was concerned at the same time with *dīn wa dunyā*, religion and world, seems difficult to understand from the general Christian viewpoint but in Muslim eyes is the precise reason why he is superior in contrast to the ascetic, 'dualistic' world-view of Christianity. Muḥammad is thus seen as the personification of the perfect equilibrium of all noble human qualities, and his spiritual way

> means to accept the human condition which is normalized and sanctified as the ground for the most lofty spiritual castle. The spirituality of Islam of which the Prophet is the prototype is not the rejection of the world but the transcending of it through its integration into a Centre and the establishment of a harmony upon which the quest for the Absolute is based. (S. H. Nasr)[3]

We must, of course, not forget that in terms of religious typology Muḥammad's place in Islam is by no means comparable to that of Christ in Christian theology. Easy comparisons have been made between the founders of the three great religions, that is, the

Buddha, Christ, and Muḥammad, although the axis of each of these religions is quite different: in Buddhism, it is *dharma*, teaching; in Christianity, the person of Christ, and in Islam, the Divine word as revealed in the Koran. Muḥammad himself is only 'a slave to whom it was revealed', as he, supported by Koranic evidence, stated repeatedly. But as God 'taught Adam the names' in the beginning of time (Sura 2:31) thus he taught Muḥammad the Koran (Sura 96:2): Muslim mystics would say that he did not teach him the external words but their content and meaning, for the Koran is the uncreated Divine word itself, which contains all the wisdom in the world. Muḥammad was called to preach this Divine word as it had been known to the prophets from Adam onward, and to announce it once more in its pristine purity, without any of the distortions that had slipped in in time or due to human weakness. For this reason, the mystics of Islam have stressed the epithet *ummī*, 'illiterate', by which the Koran describes the Prophet (Sura 7:107–108). For just as Mary had to be a virgin, an immaculate vessel to contain and to give birth to the 'word made flesh', so Muḥammad had to be free from secondary intellectual pollutions in order to be a pure receptacle for God's word that was to be 'made a book' in the Koran: 'incarnation' and 'inlibration' (a term coined by Harry Wolfson) stand in phenomenological relation to each other.

Muslims have always been aware of and constantly refer to Muḥammad's human nature and its limitations. They have never seen him as a quasi-divine or deified being; he was the messenger who was singled out to bring the eternal word. Yet a deep veneration of God's messenger grew up during the first generations of the community of the faithful. It reached mystical, and even mythical, heights in later times and would lead some people to the unorthodox idea that the night of his birth was even better than the *lailat ul-qadar*, the Night of Might: that night in Ramadan when the first revelation of the Koran took place and which is, according to the Koran itself, 'better than a thousand years' (Sura 97:5).

Muḥammad is primarily 'a beautiful model' (Sura 33:21) for a Muslim. To follow him and to imitate his *sunna*, his way of life, in the minutest detail, was the ideal of the pious. Collections of *ḥadīth*, traditions concerning his words and actions, were made from very early times, and form a most important part of Muslim literature. Thus Ghazzālī, the great theologian and moderate mystic of medieval Islam, wrote around the year 1100:

> Know that the key to happiness is to follow the *sunna* and to imitate the messenger of God in all his coming and going, his movements and rest, in his way of eating, his attitude, his sleep and his talk. I do not mean this in regard to religious observance, for there is no reason to neglect the traditions which are concerned with this aspect. I rather mean all the problems of custom and usage, for only by following them unrestricted succession is possible. God has said (Sura 3:29): 'Say: If you love God, follow me, and God will love you', and He has said (Sura 54:7): 'What the messenger has brought—accept it, and what he has prohibited—refrain from it!' That means, you have to sit while putting on trousers, and to stand when winding a turban, and to begin with the right foot when putting on shoes . . .

The *imitatio Muḥammadi* is, to use Armand Abel's poignant formulation, an imitation of action and activity, whereas the *imitatio Christi* is the imitation of suffering. The Muslim may say in his free prayer:

> We ask Thee for what Thy servant and messenger Muḥammad has asked Thee; we take refuge with Thee from that from which Thy servant and messenger has taken refuge with Thee.[4]

The *sunna* becomes a normative power, comparable, to a certain extent, to the Arabic letters of the Koran which were used wherever Islam reached; and the example of the Prophet as shown in the *ḥadīth* was imitated from Indonesia to West Africa. This explains the similarity and even the uniformity, of a number of social norms and forms of etiquette as can still be observed in the Muslim world—hence the similarity of the atmosphere in a bazaar in Afghanistan and Morocco, or of ceremonies of welcome and hospitality in a traditional home in Istanbul and one in Karachi. The conviction that besides the Koran the Prophetic tradition is the strongest binding force and the most important formative agent for millions of Muslims has led many pious Muslims to a wholesale rejection of *ḥadīth* criticism as practised by some scholars. Even a highly sophisticated Persian scholar like S. H. Nasr, who is perfectly conversant with all the intricacies of modern western science, speaks of the 'famous —or rather should one say infamous —historical method', when he discusses the various types of *ḥadīth* criticism in the West.

According to the Koranic statement, Muḥammad is the 'seal of the prophets', the last of the long line of prophets that began with Adam, and can be seen thus, like his predecessors, in accordance with dogmatic criteria. Like every prophet he had to possess the qualities of truthfulness (*ṣidq*), trustworthiness (*amāṇa*), conveyance of the message (*tablīgh*), and intelligence (*faṭāna*). It is impossible to imagine that he could have told lies (*kadhb*), or have been treacherous (*khiyāna*), or have kept his message to himself (*kitmān*), or have been stupid (*balāda*). It is, however, possible that he was subject to human contingencies (*aᶜrāḍ*). That is why the faithful can pray when visiting the Prophet's tomb in Madina:

> I bear witness that thou art the apostle of God. Thou hast conveyed the message. Thou hast fulfilled the trust. Thou hast counselled the community, and enlightened the gloom, and shed glory on the ḍarkness, and uttered words of wisdom. (*Dalīlu'l-ḥajj*)

The finality of prophethood is of central importance for Islamic theology. Muḥammad is understood according to Sura 61:6 as the *paraklet* who has come to fulfil the message of Christ. *Parakletos* is read here as *perikletos*, 'praised', a word that is associated with one of Muḥammad's honorific names: Aḥmad, 'Most praiseworthy'. Pious Muslims have looked for prophecies of his advent not only in the Old and New Testaments but also in the sacred books of Indian religions and of Zoroastrianism, and have found many a sentence that could be applied to Muḥammad. For, as R. A. Nicholson remarks in his commentary to Rūmī's *Mathnawī*:

> As the sum of an arithmetical series represents all the numbers of which it is composed, so Muḥammad, the Seal of the prophets, unites in himself the perfections of all his predecessors. Essentially they are one with him and share in the honours paid to him.[5]

The problem of the finality of Muḥammad's message is politically of great importance. A branch of the Qadianis, inspired by Mirzā Ghulām Aḥmad in India at the beginning of this century, known as Ahmadiyya, held that their founder had brought a continuing revelation. The true extent of Ghulām Aḥmad's propheto-messianic claims has been and still is a matter of controversy. The Ahmadiyya are extremely active as Islamic missionaries in the western world; they are largely responsible for building many mosques outside the heartland of Islam, and are among the most efficient translators of the Koran, although they offer a very modernistic, pseudo-scientific interpretation to the words of the Holy Book. All these missionary activities notwithstanding, the Ahmadiyya have always been viewed with mistrust by the majority of orthodox Muslims, and as a result of various inter-factional riots in Pakistan they were declared a non-Muslim minority in Mecca then Pakistan in 1974. Muhammad Iqbal, the poet-philosopher of the Indian Muslims, suggested such an action as early as 1936 in an Open Letter to Pandit Nehru. It is difficult for an outsider to define the borderlines clearly. In *Islam* by Sir Zafrulla Khan, a prominent Pakistani politician and jurist who is a follower of the Ahmadiyya, we find a chapter entitled 'Muhammad the excellent exemplar', and I cannot imagine that a single word in this chapter, written with deep, heartfelt love, and true devotion, could be unacceptable to an orthodox Muslim.[6]

As for Iqbal, whose anti-Ahmadiyya stance certainly had political reasons, he like millions of Muslims in the past and present, said that the finality of Muḥammad's prophethood was the true ground of Islam's claim to all-embracing supremacy and world rule. In his 1928 *Lectures* he explained this in his peculiar philosophic style:

> The Prophet of Islam seems to stand between the ancient and the modern world. In so far as the source of his revelation is concerned, he belongs to the ancient world; in so far as the spirit of his revelation is concerned, he belongs to the modern world. In him life discovers other sources of knowledge, suitable to its new direction. The birth of Islam . . . is the birth of inductive intellect. In Islam prophecy reaches its perfection in discovering the need of its own abolition. This involves the keen perception that life cannot for ever be kept in leading strings; that in order to achieve full self-consciousness man must finally be thrown back on his own resources . . .[7]

Muḥammad's rôle as the last and final prophet and as carrier of the complete and perfect revelation had been explicitly stated in the Koran; the same is true of his activity, which should embrace the whole world. 'We have sent him as mercy for the worlds' (Sura 21:107). Poets and mystics have often dwelt upon this aspect of his life, drawing a line between the Divine mercy as it reveals itself by sending the Prophet, and that same mercy that reveals itself in the life-giving clouds and rain (cf. Sura 7:155). Today the villagers in Iran and Anatolia call the rain *raḥmat*, 'mercy', just as the Prophet is *raḥmatan lil-ᶜālamīn*. It was easy, then, to describe poetically how he quickened dried-up human hearts with his preaching; how he poured out the water of Divine grace, and made mankind fresh and green so that they could bring forth rich spiritual fruit. Muḥammad is seen as the rain cloud that wanders from Istanbul to Delhi, from Morocco to China to refresh the souls of the faithful,[8] and popular mystical poetry in the Indus Valley describes the 'jewel-bearing cloud' as did the sophisticated Urdu poet Ghālib in nineteenth-century Delhi. It was almost unavoidable that some masters of theosophical speculation in later Islam should have interpreted Muḥammad's rôle as 'mercy for the worlds' by extending it with the idea that he was the manifestation of the Divine name *ar-raḥmān*, 'The Merciful', which is considered the highest of the ninety-nine Divine names after the name Allah.

One of the most important aspects of the veneration of Muḥammad is the formula of blessing for him; for it is said in the Koran (Sura 33:56): 'Verily God and the angels bless Muḥammad'. It was only logical that the faithful should imitate this Divine and angelic act. The blessings for Muḥammad and his family (*ṣalawāt*, *durūd*) are among the most important religious formulas in Islam, being repeated every day by millions of faithful. Even the bee hums the *ṣalawāt* when entering the bee hive, and thus honey comes into existence—at least that is how the medieval Turkish folk poet Yūnus Emre saw it.[9] The *durūd-i sharīf* has developed into a protective formula, being recited at the beginning of every work, or in difficult times, and many pious use it as their constant *dhikr*. Did not even the leading moderate theologian of medieval Islam, al-Ghazzālī, teach in consonance with the traditions that God utters ten blessings over everyone who utters once the blessing for Muḥammad? The constant recitation of this formula results in a feeling that the Prophet is always close to a faithful Muslim who directs his love and trust toward him; thus, his personality became a medium—if not *the* medium—of religious experience. His family is likewise lovingly venerated. That is true not only of the Shiites but of Sunni Muslims:

> God has not created anything that is dearer to him than Muḥammad and his family,

as the great martyr mystic al-Ḥallāj says.[10] The Prophet's descendants, the *sayyids*, still enjoy great respect and play an important rôle in the religious and sometimes even the social life of the community (intermarriage only with *sayyid* families, and so on).

Muḥammad refused any claim to have worked miracles. His only miracle was the preaching of the Divine message as revealed in the Koran. Popular piety, however, soon attributed miracles to him which through popular songs and the 'Stories of the Prophets' were so fixed in the common mind that they almost obscured his historical personality. We find such stories already in the first biographies of the Prophet; these were then embellished and enlarged, and eventually collected in widely read devotional books. Further, Muḥammad's rôle as intercessor at Doomsday was elaborated by the pious, although it can scarcely be derived from the Koran. Koranic verses, such as the 'Splitting of the moon' (Sura 54 : 1) were applied to his miraculous powers, and rich details were added to simple allusions. The tales about his birth were enlarged in particularly fantastic ways. Some of the trends in these stories, such as the appearance of heavenly light in the hour of his birth, have parallels in the birth legends of the other founders of the world religions. The Light of Muḥammad, however, became a focus of meditation in mystical circles from the eighth century onwards, as Père Nwyia has shown.[11] In the eleventh or twelfth century the pious began to commemorate his birthday on 12th Rabīᶜ ul-Awwal, the third lunar month of the Muslim year. In 1929, Iqbal mentioned the importance of the celebration of the Prophet's birthday for the strengthening of the solidarity of the Muslims in South India, and indeed, the day is still celebrated more or less intensely all over the Muslim world. Thousands of hymns and songs have been composed by pious poets in every language for this occasion. One among them has gained special fame: that is, the Turkish *mevlūd-i sherīf* by Suleyman Chelebi of Bursa, written around 1410.[12] Even now, in secularized Turkey, it is sung on the Prophet's birthday as well as on memorial days of a bereavement, and so on. Its unsophisticated Turkish words and its simple melody are always moving. Its most beautiful part is probably the great *Marḥabā* 'Welcome!', which all created being, atoms and stars, animals and plants sing when the light of the Prophet begins to radiate in the night of his birth.

> Welcome, O high prince, we greet you!
> Welcome, O mine of wisdom, we greet you!
> Welcome, O secret of the Book, we greet you!
> Welcome, O medicine for pain, we greet you!
> Welcome, O sunlight and moonlight of God!
> Welcome, O one who is not separated from God!
> Welcome, O nightingale of the garden of Beauty!

Welcome, O friend of the Lord of Power!
Welcome, O refuge of your nation!
Welcome, O eternal soul, we greet you!
Welcome, O cupbearer of the lovers, we greet you!
Welcome, O darling of the Beloved!
Welcome, O much beloved of the Lord!
Welcome, O mercy for the worlds!
Welcome, O intercessor for the sinner!
Welcome, O prince of this world and the next!
Only for you Time and Space was created . . .

Muḥammad's praise, sung by created beings at his birth, is echoed in every branch of Islamic poetry. It would be easy to compile an anthology *The Poets' Life of Muḥammad* as a parallel to Norman Ault's *The Poets' Life of Christ*. Major and minor poets of the Turkish and Persian tongues, who saw in him 'religion embodied' (thus Khāqānī, d. 1199), have written moving hymns in his honour (*na^{c}t*); they were imitated by the poets of the Indian subcontinent who did the same in Urdu and the regional languages, where even Hindus sometimes participated in the art of *na^{c}t* poetry.[13] Arabic poets have invested the Prophet with sumptuous verbal robes, the most famous one being Būṣīrī's (d. 1298) *Burda,* the 'Cloak poem', which is connected with the miraculous recovery of the poet by means of the Prophet's cloak, and which has been translated into almost every Islamic language, largely influencing devotional poetry even in Swahili.[14] It carries on the tradition of the famous *Burda* by Ka^{c}b ibn Zuhair, that powerful *qaṣīda* which begins with the words *Bānat Su^{c}ād*, 'Suad has gone', and which gained its hitherto rebellious author the forgiveness of the Prophet, who cast his *burda* over the poet's shoulders (the poets in Sind who sing eulogies of the Prophet derive their professional name *bhān* with a charming though false wrong etymology from the first word of this poem, *bānat*). Popular poets in Anatolia and West Africa, in the Afghan mountains and the plains of the Panjab, in the rugged rocks of Balochistan and on the rivers of Bengal, have praised the great leader on the path to salvation in images of their respective traditions, describing him as a merciful rain cloud, as a powerful prince, as the leader of the caravan, or as a boatsman and a pilot.

His ascension to heaven, *miʿrāj*, to which the first words of Sura 17 allude, has inspired the poets: E. Cerulli has followed the medieval Arabic tradition in his learned study *Il Libro della Scala*.[15] Hardly any major epic in Persian or related languages contains no poetical description of Muḥammad's night journey through the spheres. The miniature painters from about 1400 onward have depicted his flight on the miraculous animal Burāq with its human face; surrounded by clouds of angels the Prophet is seen soaring into the Divine Presence, where even Gabriel has no access.[16] The Sufis saw the Prophet's ascension as a model of their own mystical experience, the 'flight of the one to the One', when the mystical 'moment' was realized in which the heart, taken out of the current of created time, experienced the *nunc aeternum* as expressed in the Prophet's word *lī maʿa Allāh waqt*: 'I have a time with God . . .' Those among the pious who recognized the earthly gardens as a reflection of Paradise were happy to know that the rose had grown out of a drop of the Prophet's fragrant sweat which had fallen to the ground during his enraptured flight through the heavens.[17]

Of course, in these ascension miniatures the Prophet is always painted with his face covered; tradition did not permit the representation of human beings, let alone the Holy Prophet. To imagine his outward appearance, the Muslim can look into the *Ḥilya*, the description of his looks and qualities as offered in classical Arabic texts. Tirmidhī (d. 892) attributes the following saying to Muḥammad in his *Shamā'il-i Muṣṭafā*:

> Whosoever will see my *ḥilya* after my death will be as if he had seen me, and whosoever sees it, longing for me, God will make Hellfire forbidden for him . . .[18]

It is small wonder that beautifully-written *ḥilyas*, reproduced in print, are still being sold to the pious in the courtyards of the mosques of Istanbul and elsewhere. The idea that Muḥammad was the loving, kind friend of human beings is reflected in many songs—even cradle songs—in which he is depicted as playing tenderly with his grandsons Ḥasan and Ḥusain, around whose sad fate many legends are woven.

It is told that the Prophet did not cast any shadow, for he was filled with light:

> Your body is all light,
> and your cheek is the *Sūrat an-Nūr* (the Sura 'Light')

sings an eighteenth-century Indian mystic, following his predecessors in Islamic mysticism who had applied the sura *Wa'ḍ-ḍuḥā*, 'By the Morning Light' or the Sura 'By the Sun' to the radiant face and body of the Prophet. The concept of light made manifest through his body is theoretically an external projection of his *ʿiṣma*, his complete freedom from moral defects. Otherwise, how could he have been the moral authority for the faithful, if he had not been without sin? 'He had to be without sin, for otherwise God would have made sin a duty for the believer!'—that is how Bajūrī, the great Egyptian theologian of the nineteenth century, expresses this view.[19] The problem was, however, how to explain the words in Sura 93 : 7 'And did He not find you erring?' But then the remark about the 'opening of the breast' (Sura 94 : 1) could be taken as pointing to his purification and Divine election.

Tor Andrae has shown in his masterly study *Die person muhammads in glaube und lehre seiner gemeinde* (Stockholm, 1918) how the veneration of the Prophet became supreme forms of mystical expression. Many traditions tell of his pre-existence, of his proximity to God, and claim that he was the meaning and end of creation. The *ḥadīth qudsī* (Divine word outside the Koran) that says *laulāka* ('Hadst thou not been I would not have created the spheres') is one of the axes of mystical piety. Another *ḥadīth qudsī* that dates back to the twelfth century forms a standard motif in popular literature of the Islamic East: *anā Aḥmad bilā mīm*, 'I am Aḥmad without m, that is, *Aḥad*, One'. The letter *mīm* with its numerical value 40 is the letter of humanity, of trial and tribulation, and of mortality, but also points to the forty degrees through which man has to pass on his way towards the Lord, until only The One,

Aḥad, remains. The very name of the Prophet became an object of almost kabbalistic speculations, so that the Bektashi order in Turkey know a *mīm duᶜasī*, connected with the Light of Muḥammad as represented in the letter *m.*[20]

> Your name is beautiful, you yourself are beautiful, Muḥammad!

That is a tune that continues throughout Islamic popular poetry. The veneration of Muḥammad's name and the blessing power, *baraka*, that is contained in it has led the Turks to the practical solution of vocalizing the consonantal skeleton *mḥmd* as *Muḥammad* only when the Prophet is intended; otherwise it is pronounced *Meḥmed*. By this device one hopes to participate in the blessing of the Prophet's name without polluting it by too much wordly use.[21]

One aspect of Islamic religiosity should always be borne in mind. As high as the mystical veneration of the Prophet reached, he was always regarded as the servant of God, *ᶜabduhu*, and venerated in this very role. For the first sentence of Sura 17 says: 'Praised be He who travelled at night with His servant'. This expression led the faithful to the conclusion that there can be no higher station for a human being than that of His servant, since the Prophet himself was called by this term during his most exalted experience, that of the ascension into the immediate presence of God. That means: the most perfect man is at the same time the most perfect servant of God. In *Jāvīdnāme* (1932) Muhammad Iqbal offers a poetical description of this fact; he puts the words into the mouth of al-Ḥallāj, the martyr mystic of Bagdad (d. 922), the author of some of the first powerful hymns in honour of Muḥammad:

> 'His slave' is higher than your understanding,
> Since he is both man and essence.
> His essence is neither Arabic nor Persian,
> He is a man, and yet previous to Adam.
> 'His slave' is the painter of destinations,
> In him lies the repair of ruins.

'His slave' is both soul giving and soul taking,
'His slave' is both bottle and hard stone.
'Slave' is something, and 'His slave' is something else,
We are all waiting, he is the awaited one.
'His slave' is without beginning, without end,
'His slave'—where is morning and evening for him?
Nobody is acquainted with the secrets of 'His slave'
'His slave' is nothing but the secret of 'but God'.[22]

The veils of mystical veneration and the numerous legends which were woven around the Prophet Muḥammad have greatly influenced the religious life of millions of Muslims. However, they have also veiled the eyes of the faithful from the historical truth, and often not much more was known about the historical Muḥammad than that he lived and preached 'many thousand years ago'. This warm deep-rooted veneration is also one of the reasons for the Muslims' extreme vulnerability to attacks from outside on the personality of the last and most perfect Prophet. Rich and poor, intellectuals and illiterates, have been united in the love of the Prophet, and his presence has been experienced as a continuous blessing.

It seems typical of Muslim attitudes that the first movements in pre-modern and modern Islam to grow out of the defence against foreign influences should have been centred upon the person of Muḥammad. The stage of *fanā fi'r-rasūl*, 'annihilation in the Prophet' and union with the *ḥaqīqa muḥammadiyya*, the archetypal Muḥammad, were well known to Muslim mystics in the post-classical period, and were regarded in many orders as the true goal of the mystic. But in the late seventeenth and early eighteenth centuries Muḥammad was again regarded as the power that could grant identity to Muslims confronted with unforeseen problems. This attitude is particularly clear in Muslim India. Certain mystical circles in Mughal India, especially under the patronage of the emperor Akbar (1556–1605) had mainly stressed the first half of the profession of faith: that is, 'There is no deity but God', and had used it as a basis for their attempts at a mystical identification of all great religious systems. These attempts endangered the particular character of Islam in that they tended to blur the borders between Islam and Hinduism. But the second half of the profession of faith, that is, 'Muḥammad is the messenger of God', founded historical Islam as a system of truth by differentiating between the revelation brought by Muḥammad and other religions.

The Muslims understood at a very early date that this formula is the secret of Islam as a distinctive and structured religion and attitude of life, pointing both to God's activity and to Muḥammad's function, as W. Cantwell Smith once remarked. Orthodox circles were always aware of the importance of the second half of the profession of faith, but this importance was high-lighted once more in the beginning of the seventeenth century in India by the leaders of the Naqshbandiyya order, recently introduced from Central Asia. The then spokesman of the order, Aḥmad Sirhindī (d. 1624), attributed supreme importance to the revival of Muḥammad's teachings, even though his attempts at reform used strange symbols.[23] A fundamentalist branch of the Naqshbandiyya in the eighteenth century was the first group expressly to call itself *ṭarīqa muḥammadiyya*, the Muhammadan Path. Founded by Nāṣir Muḥammad 'Andalīb in about 1734 in Delhi, the movement was carried on by his son Khwāja Mīr Dard (1721–1785), the great mystical Urdu poet, who devoted many of his writings to a more or less systematic explanation of the Muhammadan Path.[24] The political influence of this *ṭarīqa* increased at the beginning of the nineteenth century during the anti-British struggle of the Indian Muslims, whose growing influence became evident not only in the political but also in the cultural areas in India. Sayyid Ahmad of Ray Bareilly, supported by the descendants of the great Delhi theologian Shāh Walīullāh (d. 1762), shaped the *ṭarīqa muḥammadiyya* into a cadre of heroic fighters against the powerful Sikh rule in northwestern India. They were doomed to military failure, but the movement continued as a theologico-political attitude, and was quite influential in shaping Muslim activities throughout the Subcontinent in the nineteenth century.

It is no accident that at almost the same time the Sanusiyya order which grew up in North Africa called itself a *ṭarīqa Muḥammadiyya.* As the Indian Muslims fought the British and their allies, the Sanusiyya struggled against the French and Italian attempts to colonialize North and northwest Africa. The Prophet in his aspects as fighter against the infidels, as glorious commander of his army, as an intelligent politician who gained victory even after a temporary defeat, and surrounded by a mystical halo, became the ideal of those groups who were looking for liberation of the Muslims from a network of Western influences that grew stronger every day.

We can well imagine Muslim abhorrence of critical, even depreciative, utterances by Christian orientalists and missionaries on the messenger of God and leader of their religion, the Prophet to whom they had been attached in love and devotion for more than twelve centuries. Books like the biography of Muḥammad by the Scottish orientalist W. Muir or Aloys Sprenger's *Life of Muhammad*[25]—both published in the mid-nineteenth century—induced Muslims to re-consider their attitude to their tradition, and to the lofty position of the Prophet which was apparently endangered by such publications. In his *Six Lectures on the Reconstruction of the Religious Thought of Islam,* Sir Muhammad Iqbal wrote in 1928 concerning Sprenger's remark that the Prophet had been a psychopath:

> Well, if a psychopath has the power to give a fresh direction to the course of human history, it is a point of the highest psychological interest to search his original experience which has turned slaves into leaders of men, and has inspired the conduct and shaped the career of whole races of mankind. Judging from the various types of activity that emanated from the movement initiated by the Prophet of Islam, his spiritual tension and the kind of behaviour which issued from it, cannot be regarded as a response to a mere fantasy inside the brain. It is impossible to understand it except as a response to an objective situation generative of new enthusiasms, new organizations, new starting-points. If we look at the matter

from the standpoint of anthropology, it appears that a psychopath is an important factor in the economy of humanity's social organization.

One of the decisive books in the process of Islamic self-identification as achieved by returning to the historical Prophet is the work of the Indian Shia author Syed Ameer Ali, *The Spirit of Islam, or Life of Muhammad,* which was published first in 1892 and reissued many times since. Ameer Ali showed the historical Muḥammad as a devoted Muslim sees him, and tried to prove by giving this picture that Islam is not only compatible with human progress (as his senior compatriot Sir Sayyid Ahmad Khan had done in numerous publications), but that this religion embodies the element of progress. Human progress and the development of all social virtues are personified in the Prophet, and the imitation of his relevant virtues is a duty incumbent upon every Muslim; that imitation is perhaps even more his duty than mere copying of every detail of his external behaviour. The virtues in which the Prophet excelled are the strongest ingredients for shaping a Muslim's character; they offer him everything he needs in order to fight successfully against infidelity, and to lead a life in harmony with God-given law, thus achieving the progress God had planned for his creatures.

The number of publications about Muḥammad grew after Ameer Ali's success to unexpected amounts. During the last sixty years, more books about his life have been written than in the centuries before 1900. In India, Maulānā Shiblī Nuᶜmānī (d. 1914) composed his first biography in Urdu, a six-volume work based on solid investigation into the Arabic sources. In the regional languages of the Subcontinent, work concerning the 'dear Prophet', *piyārā rasūl*, became more and more popular.

The first historical approach to a biography of Muḥammad in the Sindhi language was written by a Hindu, L. Jagtiani, in 1911, because he was worried that his Muslim students were still living in the haze of mythological and mystical ideas about the Messenger of God. He offered, in fact, a remarkably objective picture of the

Prophet according to the Persian and European publications that were available to him. The biography of Muḥammad by the orthodox Sindhi scholar Ḥakīm Fatḥ Muḥammad Sehwānī was published three years later, and reprinted several times. Ḥakīm Sehwānī regretted that his colleagues in Sind had not devoted their energy to studying the life of the Prophet but had wasted talent and time in writing frivolous novels and short stories.

The general criticism of European orientalists' studies prevails in the books published in the Middle East and Muslim India after 1850, but one work is always quoted with enthusiasm: Carlyle's *On Heroes and Hero Worship.* Few of its ardent admirers have actually read the entire essay on Muḥammad, but Carlyle's at least partly positive evaluation of the Prophet has been constantly and still is cited. Unfortunately, German literature was virtually unknown in the Muslim countries; therefore the apologists missed Goethe's *West Östlicher Divan* which contains perhaps the most beautiful and 'Islamic' approach to the Prophet's message in Western poetry, as a typical extract shows:

Und so will das Rechte scheinen,
was auch Mahomet gelungen:
Nur durch den Begriff des Einen
Hat er diese Welt bezwungen.

Thus the right thing seems to be
the way by which Muḥammad succeeded:
Only by the concept of the One
has he conquered this world.

Once more Iqbal took over into his Persian verse Goethe's allegory of the Prophet as expressed in 'Mahomets Gesang': his poem 'The River' in the collection of poems called *Payām-i Mashriq* (1924) uses the image of the living stream, which is thus brought back to its roots in the Islamic tradition, for the image of Muḥammad as a stream that carries with him everything and then returns to the ocean of God can also be found in the poetry of Muslim mystics, such as Rūmī.[26]

Indian Muslims were generally impervious to the appreciation of Muḥammad shown in some works of German literature and scholarship, and found the often positive French books on the Prophet during and after the period of the Enlightenment quite unusable. These publications were also largely unknown in the French colonial empire, or areas under French cultural domination.

At the beginning of the nineteen-twenties, one ᶜAbdul Majid Quraishi, a school-master by profession, founded the Sīrat movement in India, which aimed at acquainting the Muslims with the life of the historical Muḥammad (*sīrat* = biography). Some studies of Arabic modernist writers were translated into Urdu, and books and pamphlets about the Prophet were widely popularized. One glance through the lists of publications issued by Shaikh Muh. Ashraf, one of the most active publishers of educational and religious literature in Pakistan, suffices to give the reader an idea of how many books are being published in English about 'Life and Message of the Holy Prophet, Muḥammad, upon whom be peace', and it would be easy to add a few dozen more Urdu books and tracts to the list.

Muhammad Iqbal, too, was connected to a certain extent with the Sīrat movement, the work of whose founder he encouraged by his letters. Iqbal's love of the Prophet is obvious in all his poetical works between 1903 and 1938. Skilfully blending modernist and mystical traditions, he praises the wonderful actions of the beloved Prophet; he is a masterful interpreter of the veneration of the Prophet in the Indo-Pakistani Subcontinent. In the *Rumūz-i bēkhūdī* (the 'Mysteries of Selflessness', 1917), he sings:

> From Prophethood is in the world our foundation,
> From Prophethood has our religion its ritual,
> From Prophethood are hundreds of thousands of us one,
> Part from part cannot be separated.
> From Prophethood we all got the same melody,
> The same breath, the same aim . . .

Just as Muḥammad was the 'seal of Prophets', Muslims should be the 'seal of nations', and as he was sent as 'mercy for the world',

Muslims, too, should become mercy for the world.

It is Iqbal upon whose words W. Cantwell Smith's remark about Muḥammad's supreme importance relies. For Iqbal had summed up the attitude of a pious Muslim in 1932 in his *Jāvīdnāme* by claiming: 'You can deny God, but you cannot deny the Prophet!'

One of the tragic events of the late nineteen-twenties is part of this picture: two Muslim youths, sixteen and nineteen years old, murdered the Hindu author of a book called *Rangēlā rasūl* ('The Pleasure-loving Prophet'). They were condemned to death, but their action brought them the blessings of innumerable Muslims, as Begum Shayesta Ikramullah tells in her autobiography.[27] As for the book itself, it was only one of the anti-Muḥammad publications issued mainly by the Arya Samaj in those years in order to win converts back to Hinduism from superficially Islamized families, as J. H. Thursby has recently shown in his book on Hindu-Muslim relations.[28]

As early as 1905 Shaikh Qidwai, speaking about the miracles of the Prophet, had stated that his greatest miracle was not, as the masses tended to believe, connected with the splitting of the moon, the sighing palm tree or the speaking sheep, but consisted of the social, spiritual, moral and religious transformation of Arabia.[29] This attitude was to be the pivot of Muslim apologetical literature in the following decades. Was not Muḥammad's greatest miracle that he, a human being, could reach such a superb perfection? His personality and his personal achievements became more and more the centre of gravity for Muslim modernist theology. His exemplary qualities are sometimes colourfully depicted in anecdotal style, and sometimes simply enumerated as entries in devotional literature. As had formerly been the case mainly in poetry, the Prophet now appears in prose as the model of everything positive and beautiful; he is the paragon of kindness, generosity, politeness, friendliness, purity and patience; his love of children, so charmingly described in many popular poems, is stressed, for:

> What was the keynote of his life? It was nothing but love:

> love of God; love of mankind! . . . love of children; love of the gentler sex; love of friends, love of foe ... (Sarwar, quoted by W. C. Smith).

Those authors who fought against the growing nationalist movement saw in Muḥammad the model of anti-nationalism. Thus Iqbal, still under the negative impression of European nationalist currents, noted in 1910 in his *Stray Reflections*:

> Islam appeared as a protest against idolatry. And what is patriotism but a subtle form of idolatry; a deification of a material object ... What was to be demolished by Islam could not be made the very principle of its structure as a political community. The fact that the Prophet prospered and died in a place not his birthplace is perhaps a mystic hint to the same effect.[30]

In books written in the early twentieth century, the Prophet is depicted as modest, patient, and industrious, and W. Cantwell Smith has deduced from these qualifications that he was meant to embody ideals typical of the bourgeoisie. This Canadian scholar interprets the very interest in the person of Muḥammad as a typically liberal attitude, and as much as the 'Life of Muḥammad' literature has grown out of a protest against what was felt to be the missionary distortion of his image, it cannot be denied that this literature is parallel with Christian tendencies, for in liberal Christianity the study of the life of Jesus (*Leben-Jesu-Forschung*) tried to replace mystical Christology. It may be true that, as Cantwell Smith claims, some modern Muslims could more easily find a way to Muḥammad as a person than to dogmatic statements or mystical speculations about him.

> Those who are too modern, too intelligent, or too busy to adhere to the *sunnah* or even the Qur'an; too lax to devote themselves to God, or to socialism; can derive great emotional and religious satisfaction from their 'love of the Prophet'.

A new approach to tradition emerged from this renewed interest in Muḥammad's personality. To follow the facts as laid down in the minutest detail in the Muslim tradition seemed less important than to recognize the spirit out of which Muḥammad might have reached this or that solution of a certain problem. This approach enabled the Muslims to look more comfortably for solutions to the burning issues of modern times in the spirit of the founder of their religion.

The love of the Prophet was shown not only in numerous books, sermons, and poems in Muslim India; similar manifestations can be seen in the Arabic-speaking world, and, after 1950, in Turkey, where the popular veneration of the Prophet was never hampered by the outward changes in life and the laicism brought about by Ataturk. The modernist theologians in Egypt had certainly prepared a way for a new interpretation of prophetology; but the most important works of Arabic scholars were first published in the nineteen-thirties and nineteen-forties. Aḥmad Amīn, indefatigable apologist of Islam, wrote several articles between 1937 and 1950, in which he shows Muḥammad not only as a social reformer but as a perfect Sufi so that he is represented as the exemplar of humanity par excellence. In 1938 the Egyptian diplomat, 'Abdur Raḥmān 'Azzām, published a book on the miraculous qualities of the Prophet, and a particularly important example of contemporary interpretation is 'Abbās Maḥmūd al-ᶜAqqād's *ᶜAbqarīyat Muḥammad*, 'The Genius of Muḥammad', written in 1942. In this book, ᶜAqqād explains the ingenious achievements of the Prophet whose *ᶜiṣma* is defined as being free of moral defects:

> He entered a world that had lost its faith, and hence had lost the secret of internal peace and external order, a world that was waiting for the liberating voice of Islam. Muḥammad was the exemplar of virtues, virtues both of the preacher and the soldier; he had the eloquence, convincing power, and intensity of the preacher, and the courage, gallantry and success of the warrior. Superb in his talents and his character, he ruled his

> time as he likewise dominated later history. No event that happened ever since was the same as it would have been without Muḥammad. History before him and after him is completely different.

The style of Muḥammad Ḥusain Haikal, the former president of the Egyptian senate and one of the most learned biographers of the Prophet among the Arab Muslims, is similar:

> He had a power which can uplift humanity to the heights of the spirit, where life consists of fraternity and love, and an ambition to know everything that exists in the world.[31]

Haikal, who otherwise used psychological methods for his analyses of the Prophet's spiritual and intellectual experiences, joins here those poets who saw Muḥammad as the embodiment of Divine love, or as the one who perfected in his life the essential human quality inherited from Adam: the capacity for love (as expressed by Jalāluddīn Rumi, the spokesman of mystical interpretation, in his *Mathnawī*, Vol I, 1066). A few years ago, an Indian Muslim scholar wrote in an article on *na^{c}t* poetry, that is, panegyrics in honour of the Prophet:[32]

> The Prophet's character, as determined in the Na^{c}t poetry, presents to the world an ideal example of submission to and harmony with God's Will.
>
> Most of the Na^{c}tia poetry is related to the spiritual, moral and social values which are directly concerned with the training of the individual and the collective self of man.
>
> The chaos and the unrest brought about by the Second World War has naturally created an urge for a new world order. This is apparently reflected in the efforts which are being made on a large scale for coexistence. The first requirement of a successful new order is a change of heart. The Na^{c}t is a branch of literature which plays an important part in building up the type of character aiming at breaking the racial, geographical and class barriers.

This last sentence can, however, lead to different consequences. In 1954 Fatḥī Riḍwān, minister in the first post-revolutionary Egyptian cabinet, described Muḥammad as the 'greatest revolutionary', and ten years later Egypt's leader Nasser called the Prophet the 'Imam of socialism'. Such ideas can easily be derived from some early works on the Prophet. F. K. Durrani in India, who wrote for some time under Iqbal's influence, and had first interpreted the Prophet in a rather liberal vein, depicted him in 1935 as the founder of the new era, the great leader who had proclaimed freedom from imperialism and destruction of slavery.[33] Part of this evaluation of the Prophet in modern terms is 'his monistic morality', which does not, like Christianity with its division between the spiritual and the worldly spheres, allow any oppression of the body; there is also his constant struggle against poverty. Even a very orthodox Muslim such as Professor M. Hamidullah (whose two-volume book *Le Prophète de l'Islam* is probably the best introduction to the thought of a Muslim who combines western scholarship and traditional learning with a deep veneration of the Prophet and strict adherence to the Koran and the tradition) has devoted an article to the problem: 'Ce que pensait Lénine de Muhammad' (What Lenin thought of Muhammad) quoting some favourable remarks by Lenin.[34] The problem of interpreting the various kinds of Islamic socialism comes within this framework.

The personality of the Prophet can be interpreted in various ways. One can see in him the meaning and end of creation and attribute to him lofty mystical gifts, or stress his human perfection as a model and exemplar for the faithful; one may feel that he has done away with the boundaries of nationalism and the limitations of social classes and casts, or that he has preached a 'higher nationalism'; one may accept him as a *socialiste avant la lettre* or as the victorious leader of the Muslim armies; admire him as a loving father of his family or as a successful politician. Whatever interpretation a Muslim chooses, it will always reflect his deep veneration for the founder of Islam, the last and most perfect of religions, a person and a symbol at the same time, about whom Iqbal says:

We are like one rose with many petals, yet one fragrance.
He is the spirit of this community, and he is one.[35]

Notes

1. Wilfred Cantwell Smith, *Modern Islam in India* (Lahore, second ed., 1947).
2. A. Jeffery, 'Ibn ^{c}Arabī's *shajarat al-kawn'*, in: *Studia Islamica*, IX (1961).
3. S. H. Nasr, *Ideals and Realities of Islam* (London, 1966).
4. Constance E. Padwick, *Muslim Devotions* (London, 1960).
5. Jalāluddīn Rūmī, *The Mathnawī*, ed., transl. and commented upon by *Reynold A. Nicholson*, 8 Vols. (London & Leiden, 1925–1940).
6. Sir Zafrulla Khan, *Islam* (New York, 1962).
7. Sir Muhammad Iqbal, *Six Lectures on the Reconstruction of Religious Thought in Islam* (Lahore, 1930, &c).
8. Shā ^{c}Abdul Laṭīf, Bhitā'ī, *Risālō, Sur Sārang*; see A. Schimmel, 'The Veneration of the Prophet Muhammad, as reflected in Sindhi Poetry', in: S. G. F. Brandon, *The Saviour God* (Manchester, 1963); and *id, Pain and Grace* (Leiden, 1976), Part II (dealing with Shāh ^{c}Abdul Laṭīf Bhitā'i).
9. Yunus Emre Divani, ed. *Abdulbaki Gölpinarli* (Istanbul, 1943).
10. For the Hallajian literature see A. Schimmel, *al-Halladsch, Märtyrer der Gottesliebe* (Cologne, 1968).
11. P. Nwyia, *Exegèse coranique et language mystique* (Beirut, 1970).
12. English translation by Lyman McCallum, *The Mevlud of Süleyman Chelebi* (London, 1941); Irmgard Engelke, *Sülejman Tschelebis Lobgedicht auf die Geburt des Propheten* (Halle, 1925).
13. Several Urdu works deal with this topic. For the popular praise poetry in Sindhi, edited in several volumes by the Sindhi Adabi Board Hyderabad under the supervision of Dr. N. A. Baloch, cf. A. Schimmel, 'Neue Veröffentlichungen zur Volkskunde von Sind', in: *Die Welt des Islam*, NS IX 1964; and *idem, Sindhi Literature* (Wiesbaden, 1975).
14. *La Bordah du Cheikh al Bousiri*, ed. and transl. by René Basset (Paris, 1894). For the Swahili versions see Jan Knappert, *Swahili Islamic Poetry*, 3 vols. (Leiden, 1971).
15. E. Cerulli, *Il Libro Della Scala* (Vatican City, 1949).
16. R. Ettinghausen, *Persian Ascension Miniatures of the Fourteenth Century* (Rome, 1957, Academica dei Lincei).
17. A. Schimmel, *Mystical Dimensions of Islam* (Chapel Hill, NC, 1975).
18. Tor Andrae, *Die Person Muhammads in glauben und lehre seiner gemeinde* (Stockholm, 1918).
19. Cf. Max Horten, *Die religiöse Gedankenwelt der Gebildeten im heutigen Islam* (Halle, 1916).

20. John K. Birge, *The Bektashi Order of Dervishes* (rep. London 1964).
21. August Fischer, 'Vergöttlichung und Tabuisierung der Namen Muhammads', in: R. Hartmann & H. Scheel, *Beiträge zur Arabistik, Semitistik und Islamkunde* (Berlin, 1944).
22. *Javidname* (Lahore 1932); Engl. translation by A. J. Arberry, *Javidname* (London, 1966), and Shaikh Mahmud Ahmad (Lahore, 1961: *Pilgrimage of Eternity*); German by A. Schimmel, *Buch der Ewigkeit* (Munich, 1957). See also A. Schimmel, *Gabriel's Wing. A Study into the religious ideas of Sir Muhammad Iqbal* (Leiden, 1963).
23. Yohanan Friedmann, *Shaykh Aḥmad Sirhindi: An Outline of his Thought and a Study of his Image in the Eyes of Posterity* (Montreal, 1971).
24. Cf. A. Schimmel, 'A Sincere Muhammadan's' Way to Salvation', in *Memorial Volume S. F. G. Brandon*, ed. Eric J. Sharpe & John R. Hinnels (Manchester, 1973); and *idem., Pain and Grace* (Leiden, 1976), Part I.
25. Aloys Sprenger, *The Life of Muhammad* (Allahabad, 1851 enlarged edition); *Das Leben und die Lehre des Mohammad*, 3 vols. (Berlin, 1861–65); cf. also W. Muir, *The Life of Mahomet and History of Islam*, 4 vols. (London, 1856–61).
26. *Payām-i Mashriq* (Lahore, 1924), German verse translation by A. Schimmel, *Botschaft des Ostens* (Wiesbaden, 1963).
27. Begum Shayesteh Ikramullah, *From Purdah to Parliament* (London, 1963).
28. G. H. Thursby, *Hindu-Muslim Relations in British India* (Leiden, 1975).
29. Shaikh M. H. Kidwai, *The Miracle of Muhammad* (London, 1906).
30. Iqbal, *Stray Reflections*, ed. Dr. Javid Iqbal (Lahore, 1961).
31. Muhammad H. Haikal, *Ḥayāt Muḥammad* (Cairo, 1963).
32. Ghulam Dastagir Rasheed, 'The Development of Na^{c}tia Poetry in Persian Literature', in: *Islamic Culture* (Hyderabad, Deccan, 1965).
33. F. K. Khan Durrani, *The Great Prophet* (Lahore, 1931 and later).
34. Muhammad Hamidullah, *Le Prophète de l'Islam*, 2 vols (Paris, 1955). *Idem.*, 'Ce que pensait Lénine de Muhammad', in: *Pensée chiite* (Paris, 1960), No. 5.
35. Muhammad Iqbal, *Asrār-i Khūdī* (Lahore, 1915), Engl. transl. by Reynold A. Nicholson, *The Secrets of the Self* (London, 1920).

Further relevant books in European languages

A. Yusuf Ali, *The Personality of Muhammad the Prophet* (Lahore, 2nd ed., 1931).

Abdar Rahman ^{c}Azzam, *The Eternal Message of Muhammad* (New York, 1966).

Abdul Hamid Farid, *Prayers of Muhammad* (Karachi, 1959).

H. Haas, *Das Bild Muhammads im Wandel der Zeiten* (Berlin, 1916).

E. Littmann, *Mohammed im Volksepos* (Copenhagen, 1950).
Muhammad Ali, *The Prophet of Islam* (Lahore, 1928, Ahmadiyya-publication).
Rudi Paret, *Mohammad und der Koran* (Stuttgart, 1957).
Z. Rahnema, *Le Prophète* (Paris, 1967); translated from the Persian into English by L. Elwell-Sutton (Lahore, Ashraf, nd).
A. Schimmel, 'The Place of the Prophet of Islam in Iqbal's Thought', in: *Islamic Studies* I 4 (Karachi, 1962).
A. Schimmel, 'The Golden Chain of Sincere Muhammadans', in: Bruce B. Lawrence (ed.), *The Rose and the Rock* (Durham, N.C., 1979).
Christian W. Troll, *Sayyid Ahmad Khan. A Reinterpretation of Muslim Theology* (Delhi, 1977).
A. H. Vidyarathi & U. Ali, *Muhammad in Parsi, Hindoo and Buddhist Scriptures* (Allahabad, nd).
W. Montgomery Watt, *Muhammad, Prophet and Statesman* (Oxford, 1961).
S. A. Wahab, *The Shadowless Prophet of Islam* (Lahore, 1949).

Experience of Time and History in Islam

Abdoldjavad Falatūri

The problem of whether Muslims have thought or think historically has often been examined and discussed by western and eastern scholars. Depending upon the way the question is posed, and depending upon who poses it, we get either an affirmative or a negative answer. While Muslim authors either consciously or unconsciously adopt an apologetic approach, a Jewish, Christian, or purely western-philosophical understanding of history shines dimly through the work of most western authors.[1] In any case, whether Muslims can or should or cannot and may not think historically has serious consequences for an understanding of Islam, and for Islam's response to the intellectual and material developments of our time.[2]

The purpose of this essay is to examine the possibility of the experience of history in Islam. Clearly, 'history' is not meant in the sense of any particular philosophical or scientific approach. It is also clear that an orientation to any other definition of the notion history is to be regarded as an *a priori* judgment which forces us to face the question: with what right and for what reasons have we chosen this or that particular definition of history as a criterion for our investigation? We must first ask whether the object of our investigation stands in relation to any kind of a notion of history at all. Many examinations fail precisely in this point and not infrequently leave out of consideration the fact that not every kind of narration from the past or utterance about the future may be described as history.[3]

We should be able to circumvent these difficulties if we turn directly to the subject itself, namely, Islam, and above all to its main source, the Koran. The Koran can be understood in various ways. The historian legitimately attempts to understand materials set in time—among which the Koran itself must be included—historically and to situate them within an inclusive concept of history. One can also attempt, as our theme requires, to understand the Koran according to its own self-understanding.

It is principally the following parts of the Koran which up till now have led us to understand the Koran as a work with a particular sense of understanding history.

(*a*) Sayings about earlier prophets and apostles and their revelations.
(*b*) Sayings about nations of the past and their relation to their respective message.
(*c*) Sayings about the expected Day of Judgment.

We must, therefore, first inquire:

(*a*) Did Muḥammad have in mind any sort of history of revelation—whatever one may understand as 'history'.[2]

Does the Koran mention earlier prophets and apostles, for instance with a view to a developmental history of sacred scriptures and/or God's teachings? Or does Muḥammad intend to proclaim something transcending and independent of time?

Muḥammad's primary concern is to spread Islam (surrender to God). All men should be guided to Islam. This guidance (*hudā*) represents the program the Koran is to fulfil: 'This is the scripture which is not to be doubted (revealed) as guidance (*hudā*) for the God-fearing'.[4] (All men are essentially and primarily fitted to be directed to Islam.[5]) Occasional obstacles are secondary phenomena, which cannot impair the total objective and plan; the goal is Islam and the means is guidance to Islam. However simple and uncomplicated the goal and means as such may appear, Muḥammad's conviction that it was never otherwise is clear and absolute. From the dawn of creation, surrender to God has been the goal to which prophets and apostles were to have led man.[6] According to Muḥammad, there is no higher goal for creation and no better plan for its realization.

'And I created *djinn* and men only to serve me';[7] service is understood as an expression of devotion and surrender to God. The proclamation of this goal and the means for attaining it make up the content of every revelation; what is proclaimed as revealed may not be accomplished gradually or in steps: Surrender to God (Islam) is not something which can gradually be realized only in the course of time, through generations and races, and in response to several revelations. One either surrenders himself to God or not.[8] Likewise, the guidance to the goal is not something which is carried out gradually over the course of generations of apostles and prophets, beginning from nowhere and ending with the apex. Neither the goal nor the means stands in any kind of relationship to time, notionally or actually. They are in no traditional sense historical.

It is also impossible on the basis of the goal and means to construct a history of salvation which is gradually realized either in a Christian or non-Christian sense, neither Muḥammad nor the Muslims thought of such a possibility. For the Koran recognizes no original sin and no corresponding redemption, so that the Koran presents no salvation history comparable to the Christian tradition. But if salvation is understood, as it is in the prophetic religions, as 'the individual's encounter through faith and grace with a personal God', then salvation is contained precisely in that human surrender to God (Islam) and that divine guidance (*hudā*) which according to the Koran remains or should remain forever unaltered by time or history.[9] Accordingly, there is no reason to conceive of revelation as something temporal or historical. It is not something that is realized gradually, either in regard to its ultimate fulfilment or its content.

The question nevertheless persists: does not the Koran's mention of apostles and prophets exhibit an historical perspective and, accordingly, the historical character of revelation?

Such a conclusion is unjustified. On the contrary, the independence of the Koranic revelation is stressed by the fact that the Koran mentions a limited number of apostles and prophets in various orders of succession,[10] often interrupting the series of names by a sudden transition to some event that happened before or after it.[11] The Koran is not concerned to demonstrate a historical succession of apostles and prophets but rather to highlight the unity of the revelation transcending history, regardless of when and how it was proclaimed. No distinctions are made among the apostles and prophets and their revelations: All believe in God, his angels, his scriptures and his apostles. 'Say: We believe in God, and in what has been revealed to us and what was revealed to Abraham, Ismā^{c}īl, Isaac, Jacob, and the tribes, and in (the books) given to Moses, Jesus and the prophets from their Lord: we make no distinction between one and another among them, and to God do we submit' (in Islam) (Sura 3:84).

Discussion of the second question further clarifies the issue:

(*b*) In his accounts of the peoples of the past, did Muḥammad intend to present a history of these peoples, or was he pursuing a different objective?

When one studies the Koranic sayings about these peoples and considers the reason for their place in the Koran, one can conclude with certainty that the Koran is not concerned with presenting a historical account of these peoples.[13] It endeavours, instead, to show the immutability of the goal of creation (surrender to God) and the programme for its fulfilment (guidance). What happens then? The narration of events which took place at a particular time and in a particular place consequently serves to call attention to the existence of the Transcendent and to the uniqueness of that which is beyond history, and to warn Muḥammad's people against the repetition of the same events. As in the revelation accounts, something unusual is involved here. The events which took place in time and space are conceived of as un-historical. Punishments inflicted on earth are regarded merely as consequences of rebellion against the transcendent goal of creation, consequences which can repeat themselves at any time or place if the content of revelation is violated. The Koran's way of viewing past events is independent of time and history, but fully accords with Muḥammad's central convictions. If the historico-critical observer does not take into careful consideration the unique character of the Koran's approach to the past, he cannot but find fault with it.

The expected consequences of certain deeds and events did not always occur, at least in Muḥammad's time. Likewise, the rewards appropriate for those who contributed to the realization of the revelation's content did not materialize in a fitting manner. There must be another time determined for reward and punishment: the Day of Judgment. As regards the Day of Judgment, we must consider our third question:

(*c*) Does not this future expectation demonstrate an historical orientation in the Koran?

The Koran clearly maintains that the Day of Judgment is not the goal of creation, that is, it is not the end for which the world was created, or the end for which God might have destined man. Hence, this conviction of Muḥammad's does not lead to a conception of time in which a real or fictitious vehicle of history develops or advances consistently from one point to another. The return of men on the Day of Judgment occurs in accordance with that very goal of creation (Surrender to God) which was already achieved when the first man was fashioned by God.[14]

How are we to understand this? When the Koran treats of past events, it understands the past in an unhistorical fashion. When it announces the impending Day of Judgment, it is the future which is being treated and which by its very nature is bound to no specific point in time. For according to Muḥammad's conception, the Last Judgment could commence at any moment, even during his own life.

> Do they then only wait for the Hour—that it should come on them of a sudden? But already have come some tokens

> thereof, and when it is (actually) on them, how can they benefit then by their admonition?[15]

The unrelatedness of the 'hour' of the Last Judgment to future time and the notion that it is as a matter of fact 'supra-temporal' is unequivocally asserted:

> To God belongs the Mystery of the heavens and the earth. And the decision of the Hour is as the twinkling of an eye or even closer, for God has power over all things.[16]

The arrival of the hour of Judgment is connected with supra-temporal, divine knowledge and is understood as something which can be perceived in the present. It is not something which occurs in the future, only after a specific period of time. According to Muḥammad's notion of the hour of Judgment, it is the autonomous action of God himself which is to the fore. It is not the historical but rather the unhistorical which is decisive: that is, the enactment of the human response to the supra-temporal message of relevation, the actualization of reward and punishment as fulfilment of the same supra-temporal, unhistorical message of relevation.

The above ought not to be misconstrued. It does not mean that Muḥammad had no experience at all of time and history. His experience was, however, vastly different. The real philosophical reason for the absence from the Koran of the notion of history in the traditional sense, lies in the Koranic concept of time, for without a notion of time no concept of history is possible. The Greek term for time, *χρόνοϛ*, is translated into Arabic by the word *zamān*, which does not occur in the Koran and is not of Arabic origin. The proper Koranic expression for time is *waqt*, which is rendered by another Greek work: *καιρόϛ*. An analysis[17] of the Koranic term *waqt* shows that it does not imply progressive enactment, and that it has no regulatory character, as is the case with *χρόνϛ* (*zamān*), a character which every concept of history presumes as its basis. *Waqt* is rather spatial, a self-enclosed, static, unalterable *where* of an event. When events take place in time and space, both considered as *where*, the context of the events is merely contingent, in no sense necessary. The juxtaposition of events in a *where*-place is just as reversible as their succession in *where*-time. In *waqt*, as in a spatial where-time rather than in a linear or cyclical where-time, that is, as in an ever-present area of events, created by God, all events are independent of one another, yet have a direct relation to their omnipotent, omnipresent Creator. The Creator could have ordered the course of history in a totally different way. As Fashioner of the where-time (*waqt*) he could have allowed Noah to appear before Adam, Jesus before Abraham, and Muḥammad before all the others; and nonetheless the goal of creation, surrender to God, would not have been altered.[18] For it would have made no real difference if one preached here and another there the same enduring message.

This principle of divine operation applies as well to the rise and fall of nations and the reward or punishment contingent on response to the divine message. Divine power determines and resolves all exactly as God would have it. This resolution (*qaḍā*) and this determination (*qadar*) may not be seen as predetermination, as predestination, with 'pre' understood temporally in the context of serial time.[19] Likewise, God's determination of periods of time (*ajal musammā*)[20] resembles the exact location of events in space. For God, all time and all space are eternally present and existent. In essence, the situating of events vertically (succeeding one another in where-time) and situating them horizontally (next to one another in where-space) remain the same. This is all that can be said about Koranic time and experience of history if one insists upon describing history as the sequence of events in where-time.

Occasionally, scholars cite certain Koranic expressions as proof for the historical conception of the Koran. Among these expressions are *naba'*—to proclaim, or the proclamation of what would otherwise be hidden; *ḥadīth*—to talk about, or comment upon something, a concern, what is said, what is recounted, and so on; *dhikr*—to remember something, to call something into consciousness, and so on; *qiṣṣa*—to recount; *ᶜibra*—exhortation, reflection.[21] In the Koran, all of these expressions are intended to place normal historical circumstances in the service of the supra-temporal, immutable, unhistorical message of revelation and thereby to give them lasting value. The same is true of the Koranic word *khabar*—report, account, matter, which was later used to translate the Greek *ἱστορία*.

In summary, it may be said that in the thought patterns of the Koran a static notion of space dominates and indeed totally overshadows a concept of time whose nature is sequential. The Koran lacks a notion of time which is the necessary basis for every scientifically comprehensible experience of history. Not only does the Koran lack a conception of history in the western sense, but such a concept simply could not exist in the Koran. The Koran affords no place for it. This does not mean that Muḥammad was not able to construct and mediate such a conception of history and its basis, that is, time. His concerns transcended time and history, as his community has understood up to the present. This kind of understanding, especially of time, is directly bound up with a notion of being, motion and knowledge. It contributed greatly to the reception of Greek philosophy, and effectively restructured the western understanding of that time in accord with its own nature.[22] There is scarcely a single Greek philosophical idea that was not either directly or indirectly affected by it. I do not, however, thereby deny the possibility or actual presence within Islamic tradition of a western notion of regulatory time and of history as sequential and continuous.[23] I do, however, wish to emphasize the dominance of the Koranic thought patterns in the theory and practice of the Islamic world. From the start, there were a number of tendencies in the Islamic world which could have eventually led to an historical way of thinking, but tradition-minded Muslims have consistently disregarded them. It is only the genesis of the Koran which could and still can suggest an historical way of thinking. For every Muslim knows that the Koran was not revealed at once but during several successive years. One is also aware that the question, why does one Koran verse stand before the other and not *vice versa*, and why were all verses simply not revealed at the same time, is to be answered by pointing out that the revelation contained in each verse of the Koran corresponds to a particular situation appropriate to it. This necessary connexion with a corresponding situation and its respective context and time repeats itself as often as there are verses in the Koran—approximately 6666 times. It could be considered at least as a principle for religious decisions alongside other principles, without putting into question the revelational character of the Koran as verbally inspired. Such a consideration and conclusion is unknown to Islamic jurists (*fuqahā'*), philosophers, and theologians (*mutakallimūn*), which shows the overwhelming dominance of the Koranic way of thinking.

The Koran's doctrine of creation in six days could have been a further stimulus to historical thought.[24] Muslims could easily have developed a history of creation from it, as was done in Judaism and Christianity. These Koranic verses, however, represent a theological problem for Muslim scholars: Why should the omnipotent Creator fashion the cosmos in six days when he could have done it in an instant?

The Koranic commentators, even the highly regarded historian Ṭabarī, draw edifying lessons from it. God created the universe in six days rather than in an instant in order to teach angels and men the virtue of patience. According to another explanation, the six days of creation point to the wisdom, freedom and power of the Creator who can accomplish whatever He wills, in whatever way He wills. There are other explanations, but they have nothing to do with historical thinking.[25]

There is, however, a mystical interpretation of the six days of creation which sees them as indications of a mystical, and therefore supra-temporal, development of the Godhead itself.[26] According to this interpretation, the six days are the days of hiddenness (*ikhtifā'*) of the Creator, who hides himself behind the world of souls, and the world of bodies, both of which issue from His creative power. This hiddenness behind the external appearance of the creature, which is accomplished directly through God's creation of souls and objects, extends from the creation of Adam up to the time of Muḥammad, that is, six thousand years. Here we can begin to trace a certain notion of development.

Divine manifestation (*ẓuhūr*) begins with fulfilment of Muḥammad's prophetic office and the beginning of *wilāya*, the direct rule of God over the earth. At the end of the seventh day, the *ẓuhūr* is fulfilled with the appearance of the Mahdi. The extent to which an historical consciousness is operative in this interpretation is clear from an additional remark of the same mystic. Acting as a Koranic commentator, he writes: 'If heaven and earth (in the verse under consideration) are to be taken literally, then the six days are the six cardinal points of the heavens'. Clearly nothing historical is intended in this interpretation.

Muslim philosophers and scholars such as al-Fārābī, al-Bīrūnī, the noted historiographer Ibn Khaldūn, and others, show a pronounced appreciation of an historical way of thought. Nonetheless, in general even they lack a notion of historicity, the idea of history as 'a generic process directed to a particular goal'.

That such an understanding of history is absent in Islam is more evident when one turns from the few philosophers and historiographers who, influenced by non-Muslim thought, did indeed think, in a certain sense, historically and considers the true representatives of Muslim spirit, those who are responsible for dogmatic theology and ethics. R. Wieland undertook just such an attempt, restricting herself, however, only to modern commentators on the Koran. At the end of her highly successful examination, Wieland concludes:[27] 'The prevailing discussions up until the present, with their possible consequences of historical ways of thought, have been carried out within very modest limits.[28] Even they have turned out to be particularly problematic, in so far as they have proceeded essentially outside of the strongholds of religious scholarship. As for the *ᶜulamā* (religious scholars), there has been no perceptible movement in their ranks toward an historical interpretation of the Koran'.

It is unlikely that we shall ever perceive such a movement. We are not dealing with an issue that can be determined by the human will, open to suggestions,[29] but with a way of thought that is grounded in the Koran itself. This way of thought was expressed quite clearly at the Freiburg Symposium. Muslims vigorously opposed any reference to an *historical* understanding of the Koran which might in any way put into question the existence of Islam and its laws as proclaimed by Muḥammad.

Notes

1. I recommend the following highly informative works as an introduction to the problem: W. Braune, *Der islamische Orient zwischen Vergangenheit und Zukunft. Eine geschichtstheologische Analyse seiner Stellung in der Welt-situation* (Berne, 1960); Muhsin Mahdi, *Ibn Khaldun's Philosophy of History* (London, 1957); R. Paret, 'Das Geschichtsbild Muhammads', in: *Die Welt als Geschichte II* (1951), pp. 214–24; idem., 'Der Koran als Geschichtsquelle', in: *Der Islam*, 37 (1961), pp. 24–42; F. Rosenthal, *A History of Muslim Historiography* (Leiden, 2nd. ed., 1968).
2. For the work by W. Braune cf. Rotraud Wieland, *Offenbarung und Geschichte im Denken moderner Muslime* (Tübingen, 1971).
3. Otherwise, for the dawn of time all men would have been 'historians', for everybody, young or old, knows how to relate something from the past (whether recent or distant) and everybody projects some hope into the future, and in some way relates both past and future to the present.
4. Sura 2:2. The petition for proper guidance forms the centre of the Meccan sura, *al-fātiḥa* (Sura 1), which every Muslim must recite at least ten times a day during his prayers.
5. Sura 30:30 says. 'So set thou thy face steadily and truly to the faith, (establish) God's handiwork according to the pattern on which He has made mankind: no change in the work (wrought) by God, that is the standard religion; but most among mankind understand not'.
6. Therefore, Adam, the first man, is recognized in Islam as a prophet (Sura 2:30–39; 7:19–25; 20:117–124). Accordingly there was never a time, from the divine perspective, when divine guidance to Islam was not provided, and no time when men were not essentially prepared for and disposed to Islam, on the basis of their created nature, their inborn faculty.
7. Sura 51:56. This verse, from a Meccan sura, implies the necesity of proper guidance to the goal of the creation of humanity, which we have already mentioned.
8. The intensity of individual belief is therefore a personal matter, and a disposition of the soul, and has nothing to do with historicity or lack of it in the content of revelation.

9. Even R. Wieland, who as a historian tries to pay special attention to what seem to be historical features in the Koran (even though Muḥammad did not think in this way), says: 'In reference to Muḥammad's view of history salvation history does not mean for him a development fostered by God's words and deeds of man's possibilities for salvation, leading to a unified goal. Rather, it is a series of ever-new offers of salvation which remains ever the same in its content, in history' (*loc. cit.*, 37).

   This is, to be sure, the sort of history an historian perceives. Whether Muḥammad conceived of such a history cannot be concluded simply on the basis of the Koran's mention of earlier apostles, prophets, messengers and peoples. Why, in any case, should Muḥammad have thought of history when he proclaimed something supra-temporal?
10. Cf. for instance Sura 3:33 with Sura 6:84–87, with Sura 2:136; 3:84 with 33:7. See also Sura 4:163; 10:71–98; 12:6, 38; 21:85; 38:45; 42:13; 57:26; 87:19 etc.
11. Sura 7:59 ff.
12. Cf. also Sura 2:136; 3:84
13. No historical continuity, therefore, can be established among the peoples who were either condemned to an earthly punishment or to destruction as a consequence of their obstinacy.
14. Sura 2:37: 'Then learnt Adam from his Lord words of inspiration'.
15. Sura 47:18; cf. Sura 43:66; further 22:55: 'Those who reject faith will not cease to be in doubt concerning (revelation) until the Hour comes suddenly upon them, or there comes to them the penalty of a Day of Disaster'. The parcelling out of punishments in the present world and in the hereafter are announced and expected at the same point in time. That means, that punishment is understood as the result of disobedience; the time of the punishment is not a matter of concern.
16. Sura 16:77. The word *aqrab*, as Paret mentions in his footnote, should be translated as 'closer', not as 'shorter'; that is more faithful to both the wording and the meaning.
17. I undertook this analysis in my thesis: *Die Umgestaltung der griechischen Philosophie durch die islamische Denkweise* (*Freiburger Islamstudien*, 1976). I cannot repeat it within the limits of this essay. I therefore present some of my findings which are relevant to the questions at issue.
18. Compare the Koranic verses mentioned in note 10, which already evidence such a mixed sequence.
19. Neglecting the distinctions in notions of time, some scholars have understood *qaḍā* and *qadar* as a divine decision, which was made either in pre-eternity or at least before the creation of man. Such conceptions have given rise to numerous theological problems regarding the Koran and our understanding of its message, which would never have arisen had time been

understood as we have explained it.

20. For instance, Sura 6:2; 7:34; 29:53; 42:14
21. Besides the word *tārīkh*, which does not occur in the Koran, the Koranic word *ᶜibra* is used as a designation for history books. The purpose and meaning of the Koranic passages referring to the peoples of the past are particularly related to the word *ᶜibra*. *ᶜIbra* provokes an understanding of the fate of the peoples, and the underlying causes for their fate, a fate which Muḥammad's people would also have suffered had they given cause. Neither in the Koran nor in the tradition, however, is *ᶜibra* seen as conveying historical material, in the traditional western sense of history. *ᶜIbra* can only rightly be understood within the context of the Koranic notion of time and history.

    M. Mahdi correctly ascribes a particular significance to this Koranic expression (*Ibn Khaldun's Philosophy of History*, p. 63ff). We cannot agree with him, however, when he arrives at his understanding of history in the Koran through the use of this expression: 'It was in relation to history, however, that *ᶜibra* was most commonly used in the Koran and in the tradition of the prophet' (p. 67). The verse to which he calls attention in this context (Sura 24:44)

    > God causes the night and the day to succeed one another.
    > Surely, there is an example (*ᶜibra*) in this for those who have eyes to see,

    exhibits nothing of an historical nature. The same is true of Bayḍāwī's commentary on this verse, which Mahdi claims as confirming evidence: . . . 'It is a basis for *ᶜibra* . . . for this proves the existence of the eternal creator, the perfection of his power, the extent of his knowledge . . .' It indicates the penetration of externals into the depths of the causes which are at their heart. This is what Muhammad had in mind with his accounts of peoples of the past. His intention had nothing whatever to do with the historicity of these accounts.
22. See the work cited in note 17.
23. I refer to those Muslim scholars who were influenced by non-Muslim thought (Greek, Indian, Iranian).
24. Sura 7:54: Our Lord is God, who created the heaven and the earth in six days, and is firmly established on the Throne Cf. also Sura 10:3; 11:7; 25:59; 32:4; 50:38;57:4.
25. Cf. for instance Ṭabarī, *Tafsīr*, 2nd ed (Cairo, 1954), Part 8, p. 205; Shaikh Ṭūṣī. *Tibyān* (Najaf, 1960), Vol. 4, pp. 451 ff. Vol. 5 p. 358 ff.; Fakhruddīn ar-Rāzī, *Mafātīḥāl-ghaib*, Part 3, pp. 224 ff.
26. Muḥyī uddīn ibnᶜ Arabī, *Tafsīr* (repr. Beirut, 1968) Vol. L, pp. 438 f.
27. Wieland overlooks the fact that the bearers of the Islamic spirit are Koran commentators, precisely as Koran commentators. The *fuqahā* and

mutakallimūn, rather, have determining influence. Their books furnish an indirect yet systematic explanation of the Koran verses which are significant for their interests. As long as no historical thinking comes into play, it has no real impact on the development of the Spirit of Islam, even if here and there a Muslim interprets one or another account from the Koran in an historical fashion.

28. The text refers to the modern Muslim authors who have been influenced by western ways of thought.
29. Non-Muslim Orientalists are prone to make such suggestions, as was the case at this symposium.

How can a Muslim Experience God, Given Islam's Radical Monotheism?[1]

Abdoldjavad Falatūri

The formulation of the question immediately indicates the nature of the problem. Are we justified, however, in thinking of it as a 'problem'?

Experiencing God is a problem in Islam because, in general, Muslim philosophical and theological thought has understood God as transcending all possible categories of being, because of his absolute unity and uniqueness. God is consequently so separated from man that the most a man can hope for is an abstract, rational experience of God, provided, of course, that he has been thoroughly trained in philosophy. Such an experience can always break down once one's philosophical premisses are shattered.

Not infrequently, polemic literature has accused Islam of maintaining an abstract monotheism which so exceeds the understanding of most Muslims that it renders a personal relationship with God impossible for them.[2] The masses resort to cults which venerate various persons or objects (trees, stones, tombs, and so on). It is suggested, furthermore, that Islam teaches the experience of no existential situation that would necessarily lead to a corresponding relationship with God, as is the case in Christianity's doctrine of the Fall of Adam, or of the Redemption (cf. various parallels in Buddhism).

Finally, experiencing God in Islam is problematic, in so far as

Islam is understood as a religion of law. In such a view, man is a slave to the letter of the law, and God is at best a righteous, that is, unyielding, omnipotent, vengeful, vindictive Lord who is tied to his own immutable will. God is, accordingly, a monster who inspires fear and terror. He awaits the Judgment Day when he will manifest to men the extent of his power: Hell for you, you rebel; paradise for you, good and faithful servant!

The works of Muslim philosophers, theologians, jurists, and to some extent, ethicians have given rise to the problems involved in experiencing God in Islam. I exclude the mystics for the time being; I shall refer to them later.

Let us turn our attention to the founder of Islam, Muḥammad, who, happily, was neither a theologian, nor a scholar, nor a systematician. He did not fragment his teachings in the Koran according to various disciplines, but focused them on the true heart of the matter, the experience of God.

When we examine the Koranic material, we discover that the question posed in the title of this essay includes the answer and the problem. The experience of God is guaranteed to man precisely because we are dealing in Islam with radical monotheism: that is, with the absence of any type of mediation (by man, nature, principle, and so on) between God and man. How is this to be understood? A possible explanation emerges when we examine the concepts contained in the expression: 'man's experience of God', namely, God, man and the experience of God. Who is God, according to the Koran? 'Say: He is God (*Allāh*), One, God the Immutable. He has neither begotten, nor has he himself been begotten. Equal to Him is no one' (Sura 112). The response which rejects all anthropomorphism formulates it even more strongly: 'There is nothing that is equal to him'. This kind of negative characterization attests to the unity and uniqueness of God, and therefore to radical monotheism, but it does not indicate how one can experience such a being who transcends all that is and all that can be thought.

Quasi-anthropomorphic assertions about the God of Islam contribute just as little to a solution to our problem. That he is 'He who hears' (*as-samī*ᶜ) (Sura 2:121 and often) and 'He who sees' (*al-baṣīr*) (Sura 17:1, and often); that he possesses 'countenance' (*wajh*) (Sura 28:88 and often,) 'hand' (*yad*) (Sura 38:75 and often) and 'throne' (*ᶜarsh*) (Sura 7:57, and often) is far from asserting *that* one experiences him, or *how* one experiences him (All these expressions are meant to illustrate God's relation to his creation and are generally used by Sunni and Shiᶜa theologians to elucidate the perfection and absolute oneness of God.)

Also, man's encounter with God (*liqā'*), reported by the Koran, is to occur first on the Day of Judgment and not this side of the grave (Sura 29:5, and often). Nonetheless, it is the Koran's conviction that the opportunity is constantly granted to man to experience his God, for God is always 'nearer to him than his jugular vein' (Sura 50:16).

Among all the attributes ascribed to the God of Islam, the symbolic characterization of God's existence and his relation to his creation seems to offer the best access to the mystery of the experience of God. Here the Koran proposes an existential illustration of the divine existence which, in the course of Islamic history, repeatedly occupied Muslim philosophers and mystics, the theologians to a lesser extent, and jurists (*fuqahā'*) least of all, and which permitted quite diverse interpretations. These interpretations, however, do not concern us. Our interest, rather, lies in the Koran's answer to our problem. It reads:

> God is the Light of the heavens and the earth. The parable of His Light is as if there were a niche, and within it a lamp: the lamp enclosed in glass, the glass as if it were a brilliant star, lit from a blessed tree, an olive neither of the East nor the West, whose oil is well-nigh luminous, though fire scarce touched it. Light upon Light! God doth guide whom He will to His light. God doth set forth parables for men, and God doth know all things (Sura 24:35)

The following assertions are important: (*a*) Allah is light: (*b*) this light emits light from itself; (*c*) this light is light of the heaven and the earth, this is, of the cosmos; and (*d*) God guides to His light whom He wills.

Surely light is not meant in a physical sense. Light is mentioned in the same fashion in another context: Torah,[3] Gospel[4] and Koran[5] all possess light. Both applications of the term have something in common, both in content and in effect. The first light, God, is on the level of actuality, the authentically real, the absolute truth. The second, namely the Light in the Torah, Gospel and Koran, is the pure truth, truth on the level of faith. God, as Light of heaven and earth, is its origin and cause. The Light of true faith enlightens the one real way to the One, to God.

Both types of light emit light from themselves, precisely because they emit light in their character as pure truth, *per se*, and not by means of anything else.

The assertion that God is Light of heaven and earth (the cosmos), and the comparison which follows make it perfectly clear that we are not dealing here with any kind of pantheism. Likewise, it has nothing to do with a *physis* immanent in the world. God is separated from the world, but nonetheless connected to it (transcendence and inherence at the same time). Hundreds of verses of the Koran describe the particular ways this relation of God to cosmos takes shape. God is sole creator of heaven and earth and all that lies between. He is not only the creator of all that exists, but is, moreover, the ultimate cause of occurrences, events, phenomena which one otherwise ascribes to men, animals, plants, earth, sky, sun, moon, clouds, wind, rain, day and night. Everything originates in his action. He is, then, the Light of all that exists outside of himself. Everything comes into existence through his Light. He is not the World. He does, however, permeate the cosmos, and all that is and all that takes place. He is everywhere, without being localizable.

He is always in the present, yet transcends time. Whenever one connects him and his action with sequential, transitory time, one makes his light transitory.[6]

Man, as part of the cosmos, is also a work of God. Man's generation, birth, childhood, youth, old age, his waking and sleeping and all his other actions and operations have their origin in God. It is God who brings forth all these phenomena. 'You (meaning the believer) have not killed them, but rather God has killed them, and you (meaning Muḥammad) have not, but rather God' (Sura 8:17). Man himself, as a part of the cosmos, and all his actions come into existence only by means of the Light, through the ever-present God who alone acts and effects.

I do not need to emphasize here that the Koran equips a God so constituted with life, knowledge, power, will and other properties. What is important is to establish how the whole of creation (man included) relates to God. The Koran says: 'The seven heavens and the earth and (all) their inhabitants praise Him. There is nothing that would not glorify Him' (Sura 17:44; 4; 62:1; 64:1). Praise presumes a certain experience of God, whether one wishes it or not, as is confirmed in the Koran in another context:

> Whatever beings there are in the heavens and the earth do prostrate themselves to God with good will or in spite of themselves; so do their shadows in the mornings and evenings (Sura 13:15).

The God who alone acts and effects is experienced, praised and worshipped in his unity and uniqueness by his creation, including man,[7] regardless of whether his creatures want to or not, regardless of whether they know it or not. The Koran maintains this powerful conviction with astonishing consistency. He is the only God, and therefore he alone can be experienced and worshipped as such.

We turn now to the second question: what is man, and to the third: what is his experience of God? Building on the foundation laid above, the light in the Torah, Gospel and Koran paves the way for another experience of God. We are concerned here not with an experience of God that is determined by generation and existence which is therefore fated, but with an experience of God grounded in free will.[8] Man (in addition to the Djinn) distinguishes himself from all other creatures in that, as a living and active being, man —and this time no longer God—fulfils, or can fulfil, the purpose of creation.

> I have only created jinns and men, that they may serve Me (Sura 51:56).

The reverse side of this assertion would read: If man does not wish to serve God, he would never have been created. The purpose of his being created is solely to serve God and in this way to fulfil the end of creation.

What does 'service' mean here, and why should the purpose of creation consist in service?

Surely what is intended is not the blind servitude of a subjugated slave. Service is also not a verbal avowal of Islam. Even belief in the sense of an exclusive conviction that there is one God cannot take the place of the service intended here. Service (^{c}*ibāda*) is much more the realization of that light which Torah, Gospel and Koran possess, the enactment of Islam as the actualization of the one true light,[9] of Islam, the only true religion[10] proclaimed to all the prophets and messengers from the beginning of creation until Muḥammad.

Accordingly, the designation ^{c}*abd* (servant) for the bearer of the Light of Islam, of him who fulfils it, is the most important Koranic designation for man, not as he is, but as he should be according to the divine plan for creation. Adam, Abraham, Moses, David, Solomon, Jesus and Muḥammad were all ^{c}*abd* in the true sense. They are numbered among those who realize Islam, surrender totally and completely. The full actualization of this surrender is not accomplished through lifeless deeds, such as prayer, fasting, alms-giving, etc. It is not accomplished through one or another moral value. The fulfilment of surrender is only guaranteed when the content of the Light sent down by God is actualized in an intention and uprightness (*ikhlāṣ*) centred wholly on God.[11]

To devote oneself sincerely to God extends not only to ritual action, but rather to all human actions (which one regards as mere compliance with the letter of the law). Even drinking, eating, sleeping, walking, engaging in business, and everything that an *abd* does is included. A genuine ^{c}*abd* who accomplishes everything in a spirit of godly sincerity stands not only in direct actual contact with God, to whom he is bound in accordance with his origin and existence, and by whom he, as a part of the cosmos, is permeated, but beyond that a genuine *ᶜabd* lives *with God.*[12] He strives, in such close contact—'We are closer to him (man) than the jugular vein' (Sura 50:16)—to gain God's good pleasure (Sura 3:66) as an expression of gratitude, which man alone among all beings, as one who with God alone acts, effects, can offer to God.

The soul, not the body of a man, the heart, not the ratio, is the locus for such a continuing relation between God and man, for the encounter with God, for an experience of God which can be described neither as rational nor as empirical. It is an experience of God *sui generis*. It has nothing to do with mystical experience in the usual sense, as we shall discuss later. It is an experience of God which takes place in the actualization of the light sent by God. Man and man alone is empowered to fulfil this end of creation, for from the beginning God fashioned him as a creature who bears within himself this Light, Islam.

> So set thou thy face steadily and truly to the faith. (Establish) Allah's handiwork according to the pattern on which he has made mankind: no change in the work (wrought) by God: that is the standard religion, but most among mankind understand not (Sura 30:31).

Service, the enactment of Islam, of the Light, which is grounded in the experience of God, is not a deliverance from an existential, fated evil. Service is the unfolding of that which was imparted to man by his Creator, the unfolding of the authentic essence of existence: that is, the unfolding of the union with God which is hidden within him, the unfolding of Islam, of surrender to the one God, an unfolding which in all its phases is a fully valid experience of God. One can describe it just as accurately as a recovery of what was granted to every man from the beginning of creation, but which remained hidden, or as a rediscovery of the essence of existence, imparted to man from the beginning of creation.

The fulfilment of Islam, of the Light, of the surrender to the one God is anchored in every mature man. In the case of an authentic *ᶜabd*, it is the question of a continuous fulfilment, which is always the same (and not a fulfilment successively improving itself). This fulfilment is regularly the experience of a God, always and everywhere present.

Not everyone succeeds, of course, in attaining it fully and completely and without false starts and errors, as is clear from the example of Adam, the first man (cf. Sura 2:35–37). On his way to becoming a genuine *ᶜabd*, to finding for himself the light hidden in himself, man encounters numerous obstacles. The struggle against these obstacles, the back-and-forth movement between God and not-God, nevertheless brings about a living practical dialogue between man and God, which is an experience of God in its own right. Even in sin, in his departure away from God and towards not-God, man, endowed from creation with divine light, experiences his creator, his God.

When one considers the names, qualities, and activities which the Koran ascribes to God and the characteristics used to describe man from this point of view[13], one sees that all these point to the relationship which exists between God and man, the only creature for whom divine love is intended.[14] Love, wrath, reward, punishment, grace, and so on, are on the side of the creator and faith, disbelief, obedience, disobedience, good, evil, repentance, and so on, are on the side of man. In any case, whether confirming or denying, man cannot escape his condition of continually experiencing God, even if he rejects God theoretically or practically.

The foregoing has nothing to do with mysticism. It is simply a question of the piety demanded clearly and emphatically by the Koran (this piety, an essential element in Muḥammad's teachings, was omitted by Muslim authorities and neglected by the theologians and jurists, who contented themselves with external actions). When Muḥammad's doctrine was organized into various disciplines, piety did not receive its appropriate place. The tenacity of the mystics in their effort to see piety as the heart of their mystical method and to use it as a foundation for their doctrines, which went far beyond its roots in the Koran, has often led Muslims and scholars of Islam to the error of seeing piety as a concern merely of mysticism. It is also not a mystical interpretation of the Koran. It is, however, for the mystic a short step to transform the Koran in a mystic direction. Koranic doctrine is based, despite the contact between God and man, which cannot be emphasized too much, on the principle of the separation between God and man, as two separate entities. The mystic can and will—and it has happened often enough in Muslim history—abolish the existing boundaries between God and his most beloved creature, man, in his striving for the unification of the two types of light in a *unio mystica*, in an experience within himself of the Light. This can occur precisely because of Islam's radical monotheism, of its one and the same Light, the Light of heaven and earth, to which God guides whom he wills.

Notes

1. Beyond their speculations concerning God, the necessity of his existence, and his properties, Muslim theologians and philosophers have apparently felt no need to question the possibility and reality of a human experience of God. As a matter of fact, it is even difficult to find an appropriate Arabic or Persian expression for 'experience of God' without running the risk of encroaching upon the absolute transcendence of the God of Islam, of anthropomorphizing him. In examining our question, it is therefore imperative to proceed from the purely religious point of view of a pious Muslim, and to rely exclusively upon the Koran for our source material, without taking into consideration the difference of opinion among the Muslim sects and schools.
2. I have in mind here particularly the discussion introduced in contemporary times by Christian missionaries in Muslim countries.
3. See Sura 5:47: 'It was We Who revealed the law of Moses; therein was guidance and light. By its standard have been judged the Jews, by the prophet who bowed to Allah's will, by the rabbis and the doctors of law . . .'
4. See Sura 5:49: 'And in their footsteps We sent Jesus, the son of Mary, confirming the Law that had come before him: We sent him the Gospel; therein was guidance and light and confirmation of the Law that had come before him . . .'

5. See Sura 4:174: 'O mankind! Verily there has come to you a convincing proofs from your Lord: for We have sent unto you a light (that is) manifest . . .'
6. See A. Falatūri, here, p. 63 ff.
7. Actions such as praise, prostration, worship, and so on, presume will and consciousness on the part of the performer. Does the Koranic conviction that there is nothing 'which does not praise Him' imply a certain animate nature of the cosmos and all that it contains? If not, how should lifeless objects offer praise to their Creator? This precise problem has been intensively discussed by Muslim scholars from various points of view. I maintain that there is an intrinsic connexion between this conviction and the other Koranic conviction that everything which exists outside of God is in reality a sign (*āya*) which continually points back to God. In virtue of its very existence, which is dependent upon God, every creature, as creature, points back to its creator. Every creature manifests its submission to its exalted Creator through the fulfilment of the works assigned to it in accord with its nature. Every creature pays homage to the perfection of his Lord (*rabb*) through the wonder of creation in which every creature shares. The Koran maintains this conviction all the more intensively, when it describes the divine reality as Light, whose activity permeates all creation, which represents at the same time an experience of God by his creatures in accord with their nature.
8. How can man's will be free, given the all-pervading character of God's action? We are touching on a problem that has from the start provoked much serious discussion among Muslims. The way one resolved this problem even became the criterion according to which Islam's first theological schools were names: *Jabriyya* (representatives of divine control) and *Qadariyya* (representative of free will). Likewise the later schools also were forced to accept one or the other solution, or a compromise position (cf. the Ash'arites and Shiites, each in their own way).

   The Jabriyya position is supported by the Koran's conviction that God is He who alone acts and effects. Further explicit confirmation can be found in the Koran: 'God created you and all that you do' (Sura 37:96; cf. 53:39). The obligation imposed by the Koran and emphasized in the tradition to pray and observe commandments with punishment and reward as consequences, supports the Qadariyya position. Such obligations obviously presume freedom of the will, otherwise they would be self-contradictory. The Koran confirms: 'On no soul does Allah place a burden greater than it can bear. It gets every good that it earns, and it suffers every ill that it earns . . .' (Sura 2:286).

   In contrast to the two opposing theses, and to the compromise solutions of the Ash'arites and Shiites, the Koran itself, it seems to me, offers a different solution, which corresponds to the God-man relationship I have outlined above. A thorough study of the names and deeds which the Koran and the tradition ascribe to God demonstrates that, according to the Koran, the God who acts in and through all is the author of all events and actions; even the actions we regard as negative are ascribed to him: for instance, that he 'hatches plots' (Sura 3:54), that he deceives certain men (for example, Sura 44:88). There is only one activity which is, by definition, not ascribed to the sole activity of God, that is, service of God, which is the object and goal of creation. Should a convinced Muslim ever accept as possible the notion that God worships himself (*'abada nafsahu*), he would be compelled to regard the whole of creation as absurd. For if God could serve himself, the creation of jinn and man would have been unnecessary. If we accept this exception we can understand man's obligation to service and every other activity as presuming freedom of will with no contradiction. In this way, the arguments of the Qadariyya and the Jabriyya can stand without contradicting one another (as it has always been assumed they must).

For a general view of the problem, cf. W. Montgomery Watt, *Free Will and Predestination in Early Islam* (London, 1948); H. Stieglecker, *Die Glaubenslehren des Islam* (Paderborn, Munich & Vienna, 1962), pp. 97 ff.

9. Cf. Sura 39:22: 'Is one whose heart Allah has opened to Islam, so that he has perceived enlightenment from Allah . . .'
10. Cf. Sura 3:19: 'The religion before Allah is Islam (submission to his will). Nor did the people of the book dissent therefrom except through envy of each other'.
11. Cf. Sura 39:11: 'Say: Verily I am commanded to serve Allah with sincere devotion, and I am commanded to be the first of those who bow to Allah in Islam'.
12. Sura 2:153; cf. 5:11, 29:69, and so on.
13. From the perspective of the actual God-man relationship and the possible man-god dialogue.
14. In my study of the names of God, of the characteristics of his nature and activity, when I proceed from the God-world relationship, as the Koran gives us every reason to do (in that it metaphorically describes God as Light of the cosmos), we can reasonably maintain that every name and attribute of God consists of an instance of what the Koran proclaims about the reality of his nature in its light metaphor.

For a general view, see the article *al-asmā al-husnā*, in: *Encyclopedia of Islam*, 2nd ed., I, pp. 714 ff; G. C. Anawati, 'Un traité des noms divins', in: *Arabic and Islamic Studies in honour of H. A. R. Gibb* (Leiden, 1965); al-Ghazālī, *al-maqṣad al-asnā fī sharḥ ma'ānī asmā Allāh al-ḥusnā*, ed. F. Shehadé (Beirut, 1971).

Characteristics of a Christian Concept of History

Raymund Schwager

It has become commonplace today to contrast the Judaeo-Christian understanding of the world with a Graeco-oriental approach. The latter, it is alleged, conceived of the life of peoples and of the processes of nature as cyclic repetitions. The Judaeo-Christian tradition, on the other hand, is seen to be the first and only tradition to have worked out a linear understanding of events affecting men. It is, accordingly, responsible for fashioning a proper understanding of history. As justifiable as these distinctions may be, they are to be applied with discretion. The Judaeo-Christian concept of the world cannot be described as exclusively linear. Within the Judaeo-Christian tradition, the yearly celebration of the great feasts, in which the decisive salvific events are recalled and thereby made present, play a central rôle. Conversely, the Graeco-Oriental tradition contains at least the beginnings of a certain linear notion of history in, for example, the idea of the golden, silver, bronze and iron ages, which follow another.

At the latest, with Herodotus, a consistent account of history arose in which events were presented as they occurred in the course of time. Greek historians, however, were not interested in the particular event as such, but in what conformed, what was regular. They considered history in analogy to events in nature. In its extreme form, cyclic thought would posit the return of Socrates and the city of Athens in their individuality.[1] In general, however, the cyclic movement of history should not be understood as a purely mechanical repetition, but as the return of what is the same but manifested in new individuals and in new constellations. People whose pattern of thought gravitated toward the universal considered this constant newness of what was essentially the same to be rather unimportant. Nonetheless, the notion of newness was at least at the periphery of their consciousness.

A sketchy comparison with modern concepts plainly indicates how unsatisfactory the cyclic-linear distinction is for clearly differentiating the Judaeo-Christian from other ways of understanding the world. Since the Enlightenment, history has become a major theme in modern thought. Very linear concepts of historical development have emerged in the work of a number of thinkers, based on the idea of continual progress and under the influence of the natural sciences' notion of time as continuously elapsing and absolute. These thinkers themselves admit that such concepts can no longer be understood as Christian. Karl Löwith impressively demonstrated in his *Weltgeschichte und Heilsgeschichte*,[2] that all modern western concepts of historical reality are indebted to the Judaeo-Christian tradition for that which is most characteristic of them. Indeed, they are essentially secularized transformations of the Judaeo-Christian tradition. Nonetheless, it cannot be denied that forms of a linear understanding of history which are not, or no longer, Christian can exist.

The conviction that what occurs in the world may not be seen simply as a process proceeding according to its own laws, but rather must be referred back totally to God, is constitutive of the Christian conception of history. Not every theological reflection, of course, is specifically Christian. Christian faith requires that God should be believed in as the God of the covenant. This implies that divine action in the world is not something which is simply accomplished with no reference to men, but that it addresses men and challenges them to recognize their own responsibility for historical reality. A Christian understanding of history insists, therefore, that man bears responsibility for the historical reality in which he finds himself involved and indeed bearing responsibility before God. Accordingly, this view, grounded in faith, is to be distinguished from all those conceptions of history which see the destiny of individuals and whole peoples as determined by the immanent laws of nature or by divine activity and which make no reference to human freedom. From this point of view, whether events in the world are conceived of as cyclic, or as more linear in the sense of a notion of decline and advance, is a secondary consideration. What is decisive for the Christian understanding of history is that God should be believed in as the ultimate ground of all this worldly reality; as a God who is personally committed, who does not carry out his plans without regard for man, but who imparts his designs to men and in this manner inserts himself into history.

The comprehensive nature of God's activity and man's subsequent responsibility is evident in the Old Testament. Wars among nations and even 'natural catastrophes' are not understood as occurring according to the blind laws of nature but are seen as punishments for man's failure to take his responsibilities seriously. By their announcement of the day of Yahweh, the Day of Judgment, the prophets make it clear that no one can escape responsibility. Old Testament faith leaves no room for chance or for blind laws of nature or history. It relates everything to the responsibility of man. This responsibility is not merely a demand which the individual imposes upon himself; instead, it represents his decision before God for salvation or for damnation.

In the New Testament, Jesus addresses himself to this same responsibility in his proclamation of the end of time and of the coming of the reign of God. Jesus did not present the reign of God as a process which would emerge of itself, but as a present reality which calls men to decision. As the Old Testament prophets before him had done, Jesus makes it plain by his announcing the impending judgment of God that no one will be able to escape this decision. In contrast to the Old Testament, however, the New Testament does not understand judgment as an event which will take place at the end of the world's history. The division which judgment effects has, according to the Christian point of view, already begun in the very coming of Jesus, and will extend—although in a way that cannot be examined in detail—through the time which still stands before us. The end of all things and, with it, the ultimate action of God, is already present and irresistibly effective within history. We can deepen this Christian understanding of history if we take note of two objections easily put forward against the Christian understanding as we have briefly sketched it: 1. Surely man is hopelessly overburdened if he must bear the responsibility for history. 2. Surely it is necessarily the case that anthropomorphic all-too-human images are projected onto God if historical events are interpreted as acts of God.

1. Like men everywhere and at all times, the men of the Old Testament learned by experience that again and again things did not happen as they would have wished them to happen. They were never able for any substantial length of time to structure the course of history according to their own wishes. They interpreted this to mean that the people had been unfaithful to God and hence had to be punished. Foreign nations who attacked Israel were seen as a scourge by which God disciplined his rebellious people. Again and again, the prophets summoned the people to conversion, so that they might one day enjoy the prosperity God promised them. The long and bitter experience that these repeated calls to conversion came to nothing eventually led to the insight that the human heart had become totally hardened, and was of itself unable to respond to God and in any positive sense to bear its responsibility for historical reality. Messianic expectation arose as a response to this insight. It was hoped that God would, in a new and decisive way, intervene in history and so transform the human heart that it might finally be able to hear God's call. This messianic expectation gave expression to the hope that at least in the future faith's conviction of man's overall responsibility would be led to correspond to actual historical experience, thanks to the powerful action of God.

The appearance of Jesus radically altered messianic expectations. No doubt his followers hoped at first that he would bring about changes in the external course of history that would correspond to the old and glorious promises. From this perspective, Jesus' mission ended as a fiasco. But this was not final. It was precisely in this apparent failure of Jesus, however, that the disciples and Christians of all ages learned to see God's decisive act of salvation and that redemptive act which freed them for authentic responsibility. Redemption and liberation in the Christian perspective do not mean that believers who regard themselves as capable of completely determining the external course of history by their free decision, and therefore as capable of carrying out their comprehensive responsibility. They mean that by Jesus' surrender to his destiny and to his death men are enabled, *despite their enduring weakness, and indeed even in their failure,* to accept responsibility for what goes on in the world.

When Christians speak about the saving act of Jesus, they express the conviction that God does not act without reference to men, despite their fundamental weaknesses. Rather, Jesus alone accepted responsibility for the historical actions of all men. In him we find the total correspondence between God's call and man's response. Christian redemption does not mean, therefore, an escape or release from responsibility, but rather the empowering of man to accept and carry out responsibility precisely when his own resources are exhausted.

The expression 'to empower for responsibility' should not, however, be misconstrued. It does not mean that believers are given a supplementary dose of moral strength to help them remain faithful to God's commands. Christians have never possessed such a total moral strength, and never will. Redemption enables man to accept and recognize his responsibility even in his failure. Although each believer is challenged to strive according to his understanding and abilities, his actions are not measured according to moral success. What is decisive is that he should affirm and accept himself with all of his weaknesses and his neighbour with all of his needs. Acceptance of responsibility and moral success are not identical in the Christian view. It is still imperative that the individual should make a decisive moral option, but he has been freed from the pressure and excessive burden of achieving success.

The Christian understanding of responsibility offers the answer to the second question posed above: Does not belief in God's activity in history lead to the projection of anthropomorphic images onto God? As a matter of fact, many of the images of God in Jewish and Christian scriptures are quite anthropomorphic. If one did not situate them in their contexts, suspicion of such a projection would be quite justified. In reality, however, precisely these anthropomorphic images of God led to a history of profound faith. Whenever the activity of God is spoken of expressly, sooner or later it is shown unequivocally that the actual course of history does not correspond to what men imagined. Frustrated expectations pressed the people to ever new decisions. Some therefore, abandoned their traditional faith. Time and time again, the prophets decried the people's turning away from the true God to idolatry. The disappointments by and large, however, led to a progressive purification and re-interpretation of traditional images of God's activity for his people.[3] This process is best illustrated by an example. The establishment of the Davidic dynasty in c. 1000 BC was seen, after some minor opposition, as an irrevocable act of God. According to the prophecy of Nathan, God had promised David:

> I will be his father and he shall be my son. When he commits iniquity, I will chasten him with the rod of men, with the stripes of the sons of men; but I will not take my steadfast love from him, as I took it from Saul, whom I put away from before you. And your house and your kingdom shall be made sure for ever before me; your throne shall be established for ever (2 Sam 7:14–16).

The dynasty, which was to endure forever, had ended definitively in 587 BC. The believing Jew faced a severe challenge to his faith. Was God false to his promises? Had his promises come to nothing? These piercing questions find expression in Psalm 89 in which the speaker complains before God:

> Thou hast said 'I have made a covenant with
> my chosen one, I have sworn to David my servant:

I will establish your descendants forever
and build your throne for all generations . . .
If his children forsake my law
and do not walk according to my ordinances,
If they violate my statutes,
and do not keep my commandments,
Then I will punish their transgression with the rod
and their iniquity with scourges;
But I will not remove from him my steadfast love,
or be false to my faithfulness . . .
Once for all I have sworn by my holiness;
I will not lie to David.
His line shall endure forever,
his throne as long as the sun before me.
Like the moon it shall be established forever;
it shall stand firm while the skies endure'.
But now thou has cast off and rejected,
thou are full of wrath against thy anointed.
Thou hast renounced the covenant with thy servant;
thou hast defiled his crown in the dust.

'Once you promised David faithfulness for ever, *but now* you have rejected him.' To this bitter question and complaint the Psalmist knows no answer. Despite frustration and disappointment, faith in Israel never died out. The destruction of Jerusalem and the Babylonian exile brought about a deepening of the traditional faith. Hope became lively and strong that God would establish a new kingdom and that a sprout from David's stock would, as Messiah, inaugurate the coming kingdom. The old promise and the old belief that God had acted irrevocably for Israel through the establishment of David's dynasty was not disregarded as false, but was indeed stripped of many external accretions. The promise which Jewish faith had at first understood as a definite guarantee for the perpetuity and prosperity of the Davidic line had to be interpreted anew in the light of unexpected events in Israel's history. Israel came to believe that the Messiah, who would establish God's final and glorious reign, would descend from David's line.

The process of purification and reinterpretation of traditional beliefs on the basis of contemporary historical experience continued in the New Testament. Jesus appeared proclaiming the reign of God and went so far as to claim that God's reign had already dawned in Jesus' own ministry. Jesus' followers first understood his proclamation in the sense of an imminent breaking-in of the long-awaited glorious reign of God, probably with Jesus as the long-awaited Messiah of God. Once again, however, events turned out otherwise. Jesus established no glorious kingdom; instead he suffered an ignominious death on a cross. The crucifixion of Jesus led his disciples to understand the reign of God in an entirely new way. The promise to David is no longer related to an earthly kingdom, but is seen as fulfilled in the resurrection of Jesus, and in his activity as the glorified Son enthroned at the right hand of his Father.

I have presented this development within the Judaeo-Christian faith in a schematic fashion. My intention was to extract one line of development from the rich variety of history and in this way to illumine a basic process. Although the actual historical development, with its secondary and even contradictory tendencies, was far more complicated, the process I have outlined corresponds to what did indeed take place in the New Testament's developing its main line of thought from Jewish tradition. The question obviously remains open whether the disciples' reinterpretations were justified and proper. An examination of this problem, however, would exceed the bounds of this essay.

The series and variety of new interpretations makes it abundantly clear that when Christian faith speaks of God's actions in history it in no wise intends to imply that it possesses a comprehensive overview of the divine plan. Christian faith, rather, confesses its belief in a God who cannot be controlled. This confession is not essentially grounded in the general philosophical recognition of the incomprehensibility of God. It is based on the experience of faith in God's action in history, that divine ways are totally other than human plans. It expresses the repeated experience in the Old and New Testaments and in the lives of believers, by which preconceived notions of God are negated. The sufferings and disappointments of a long history are involved in this process. Belief in the action of God in history, accordingly, by no means led to an anthropomorphic conception of God. It served to give added existential weight to confessions of God's incomprehensibility and absolute otherness. History was relieved of the temptation to try to control God's activity.

The central Christian confession, that God acted definitively in Jesus, may not be dealt with in isolation. It must be understood in the context of all those experiences which testify to God's incomprehensibility and his absolute autonomy. Belief in the breaking-in of God's reign through the works and person of Jesus does not therefore enable Christians to judge history definitively. The reign of God can be equated with no historical entity, neither with the Church or churches, nor with any 'Christian' government or empire. It may not even be limited to those who expressly confess Jesus as the Messiah of God. It is not a kingdom of believers, but the kingdom of God; and God as he who cannot be manipulated. He is not bound down in his actions to any external confessions on the part of man.

It may appear to non-Christians to be contradictory when, on the one hand, the unqualified claim is made that God acted definitively in Jesus of Nazareth and when, at the same time, it is asserted that the decisive action of God affects all men. From the Christian point of view, this tension is resolved by the conviction that the definitive act of revelation and salvation is to be seen in the condemnation and crucifixion of Jesus. In other words, the historically visible figure of Jesus is confessed as the absolute sign of God's action in history, exactly in so far as it is negated as an external and visible figure. As the crucified, Jesus is the rejected, the nameless. Belief in the definitive action of God in Jesus does not provide Christians with any handy criteria for drawing demarcation-lines in history. Christianity holds that Jesus as the nameless identified himself with all the nameless of humanity, and that the definitive form of God's action can be discerned in all who are rejected by the world.

Just as Jesus is the decisive sign of God's activity in so far as he is denied as an external historical figure, so his time is the definitive time in that through his coming the external, linear time scheme is abolished. Jesus claimed that time was fulfilled, that the hour of fulfilment had come. What Jewish prophets and holy men had promised and awaited was now present reality.

Since history continues after Jesus and the visible end of the world as expected by many has not occurred, the fulness of time cannot be understood in a linear-chronological sense, but in an eschatological sense. 'Eschatological' means here that whenever a man opens himself up to the activity of God, he enters into the fulness of time. The Christian does not understand this fulness as a segment of time to which one could look back, as to an event which took place in time two thousand years ago. The fulness of time, understood eschatologically, is a dimension of existence in faith, by which it becomes contemporary with the time of Jesus. The Protestant theologian Rudolf Bultmann could therefore say: '... in early Christianity history is swallowed up in eschatology'.[4]

This position is admittedly somewhat one-sided. With all its emphasis on the preciseness and present reality of the reign of God, the New Testament never fully screened out the dimension of a future within the world. Bultmann correctly, however, calls attention to the fact that the linear-chronological understanding of time, which so many people have characterized as typically Christian, was breached by the coming of Jesus. Time continued after his death, and the expected imminent end did not take place. The disillusionment caused by these two factors did not, however, lead to a deeper crisis, for the temporal-chronological components were no longer decisive. Very early on, Jesus' disciples understood his death and resurrection as an all-inclusive salvific event and as a universalization of the promise made to Israel. The action of God was no longer considered to be limited to Israel but was believed to be active and effective among the Gentile nations as well. This expansion was never, however, understood so as to identify the reign of God with the history of the world.[5] Both are separate realities, but the reign of God is nonetheless present everywhere in the history of the world. The Christian churches are a visible sign of this present reality. They too are not to be equated with the reign of God, but point to it and work in history as agents of discernment and challenge.

Since Christian faith confesses that God acted definitively in Jesus and through him extended his reign over all humanity, the 'time after Jesus' can claim no new theological dimension as appropriate to itself. This segment of history is not structured with a view to a new intervention by God. The final judgment is a this-worldly event, in that it is already present and effective. The time which is still current should be thought of rather as a 'space' in which each man can still attain to that fulness of time which Jesus Christ has already opened up for us. An individual man, an individual believer, may live chronologically after the time of Jesus Christ but, in the depths of his being, he is still on the way to fulness of life.

Notes

1. Chrysippus says: 'Socrates and Plato will exist again and every man with his friends and his fellow citizens; he will suffer the same and do the same. Every city, every village and field will grow again. And this restoration will not happen once, but the same will return without limit and end' (quoted by R. Bultmann, *History and Eschatology*, Edinburgh, 1957, p. 24).
2. Karl Löwith, *Weltgeschichte und Heilsgeschichte* (Stuttgart, 1953).
3. G. von Rad, *Old Testament Theology,* 2 vols. (Edinburgh, 1962, 1965).
4. R. Bultmann, *History and Eschatology, op. cit*., p. 37.
5. Hegel was the first to identify the Kingdom of God with world history.

Relations with Unbelievers in Islamic Theology

Peter Antes

Christian-Muslim dialogue can only be pursued objectively when it is clear to the Christian partner that for the Muslim there are certain Koranic and theological associations which relate Christians to unbelievers and occasionally treat them as a single group. It is my task here to analyze these associations to some extent. I first recall the many-sided notion of the unbeliever (*kāfir*), then point to tolerance and intolerance in Islam, and finally discuss the nature of unbelief (*kufr*) and its important consequences for Muslim-Christian dialogue.

1. *The notion of the unbeliever* (kāfir)

In Koranic usage, Kāfir means first of all 'ungrateful',[1] and later 'unbelieving' in the sense of non-Muslim. This last meaning sheds light on Islam's concrete relation to well-known non-Muslim groups of its time. Most significant for the problems of Muslim-Christian dialogue is Islam's relationship to the *Ahl al-Kitāb*,[2] the 'people of the book', that is, Christians and Jews, who claim to be recipients of a revelation,[3] which from the Muslim point of view was completed and, where necessary, corrected by Muḥammad. The idea that there had been many successive revelations and that the revelation given through Muḥammad was final and definitive because it was set down in writing, implies approximately the same sort of relationship between Islam and Christianity as had obtained between Christianity and Judaism; Islam is regarded as the 'perfection and completion'[4] of previous revelation in Christianity. Christians and Jews are called people of the book because they claim to hand on what has been set down in written form, that is, *Injīl* or *Taurāt*. According to Islamic doctrine *Injīl* is the proclamation of Jesus or, as a book, the documentary account of the proclamation of the historical Jesus. Islam contests the claim that the widely-differing gospels of the New Testament represent an authentic account of Jesus' message. A similar position is taken by Islam vis-à-vis the proclamation of Moses (*Taurāt*) and its relation to the five books of Moses.

Kāfirūn or *kuffār* refer to all who rejected the prophet Muḥammad, that is the unbelievers of Mekka. Islam holds that at the Day of Judgment God will condemn them and banish them for eternity to hell. This threat of punishment gradually sharpened Islam's position toward unbelievers. Islam rejected and opposed both the people of the book and polytheists[5] in various degress of harshness. Yet, it is said:

> Those who reject (Truth) among the People of the Book and among the polytheists, will be in hell-fire, to dwell therein for aye, they are the worst of creatures. Those who have faith, and do righteous deeds—they are the best of creatures.[6]

Whereas the Koran describes only non-Muslims as 'unbelievers', later polemic within Islam applied this term to Muslims who represented the opposition opinion. Eventually, every divergence from *ijmā*ᶜ, the 'consensus patrum', was regarded as 'unbelief' (*kufr*).[7] This extension of terminology gradually led to a formulation of various categories of unbelief. The *Lisān al- ᶜarab*, for example, lists the following:

(*a*) *Kufr al-inkār*. This variety of unbelief is to be ascribed to those who neither know nor believe in God.

(*b*) *Kufr al-juḥūd* presumes knowledge of God, which, however, finds no response in the profession of faith. Although these *kuffār* know very well what is true, they continue to deny what they know and affirm what is false.

(*c*) *Kufr al-mu^{c}ānada* situates unbelief within man. Knowledge and confession of faith are presumed. Such a man is an unbeliever, however, because, inwardly, he stubbornly refuses to accept the truth which he himself has recognized.

(*d*) *Kufr an-nifāq*, finally, refers to hypocrisy.

With the exception of the first category, the *kufr al-inkār*, all the other categories are grounded in the exercise of the will. Denial (*juḥūd*), obstinacy (*mu^{c}ānada*) and hypocrisy (*nifāq*) are the characteristics of the remaining categories of unbelief. Is it any wonder that God punishes such men, just as a human father would his defiant son? Even though God is never called Father in the Koran and the comparison can therefore easily be attacked, many features of Islam's image of God justify comparing his position to the dominant rôle of the father in the oriental family. Considering the various emotional associations connected with the word 'father' almost everywhere, applying such a term analogously to God perhaps hinders rather than facilitates a proper understanding of God. It would therefore not only be unkoranic, but also inappropriate.

It is in any case quite clear that God harshly judges all who knowingly reject his truth. We must examine the dimensions of his judgment. Men cannot be allowed to oppose what is for their own good. One should desire and endeavour to deliver them from error and so to preserve them from the fire of hell. If unbelievers cannot be brought to their senses, should not God's faithful servants see to it that judgment and punishment are meted out even in this world? We are touching now upon the serious issue of tolerance and intolerance in Islam.

2. *Tolerance and Intolerance in Islam*

R. Paret[9] described in detail and comprehensively the inner-Koranic development of Islam's relationship to non-Muslims. He showed how Muslims at first only gradually distanced themselves from Jews and Christians when both groups continued to refuse to recognize Muḥammad's prophetic office. In contrast to polytheists, the 'peoples of the book' enjoyed certain protections.[10] They were and are even now permitted to practise their religion freely within the Dār al-Islām, provided they do not proselytize directly. Altercations with Christians and Jews ensued on the one hand when Koranic commentaries and systematic theologians discussed the issue of *kufr*; on the other hand when they analyzed the contradictory currents within Christianity, and when they studied the New Testament, especially comparing the four Gospels. Seldom, however, did such texts and studies fall into the sort of unrestrained polemic which we find in the popular literature.

3. *The Nature of Unbelief* (Kufr)

(*a*) The Koranic commentary of Ṭabarī (d. AD 923) may well be regarded as the most significant of the ancient commentary-compilations. Ṭabarī provides a running commentary to the verses of the Koran, explaining an individual verse, word or group of words without however formulating a total system on the basis of Koranic doctrines, as the systematicians try to do.[12] When we examine the passages in the commentary which relate the peoples of the book to pagans and/or unbelievers,[13] it is clear that Ṭabarī sharply distinguishes the peoples of the book from the polytheists (*mushrikūn*). He expresses a decidedly higher opinion of the peoples of the book.[14] The sins which are grievous in Muslim eyes are mentioned by Ṭabarī when he comments upon Sura 3 : 110. They are associating anyone or thing to God (*shirk bi-llāh*)[15] and calling the prophet a liar (*takdhīb*). But what should be said (*a ᶜẓam al-ma ᶜrūf)* is: There is no God besides God. Ṭabarī writes: 'If the people of the Torah and the Gospel among Jews and Christians were to recognize that Muḥammad—God bless and save him—and the message he brings them from God are true and worthy of belief, it would be far better for them in God's sight now in this life and later in the next. "There are believers among them" means: among the peoples of the book, among Jews and Christians, there are believers who regard the Apostle of God—may God bless and save him—and the message he brings them from God as worthy of belief'.[17] Then Ṭabarī mentions the names of a few such believers. He asserts quite simply and without polemical rhetoric that the majority, however, of the peoples of the book are transgressors because they refuse to accept Muḥammad.

Despite the variety of interpretations of Sura 3:1–9, a few people of the book are able to be saved without formally accepting Islam.[18] Since all explanations depend upon the various interpretation concerning the occasion for the revelation of this verse, the otherwise encouraging statement is of little practical use in the contemporary dialogue with Islam.

On the Christian side, an obstacle to dialogue is the Christian belief in the divinity of Jesus Christ. Accordingly, 'they (Christians) have wandered from the path of salvation'.[19] Ṭabarī in his explanation of Sura 5:17[20] treats exhaustively of the error of regarding the Messiah as God. In another place, he emphasizes, in contrast, Islam's basic openness to further historical revelations, that is beyond the Torah and Judaism to Jesus, and beyond Jesus and the Gospel to the Koran proclaimed by Muḥammad.[21] Even if 'these unbelievers among the Jews and Christians from the Sons of Israel regard him as a liar', he should not be distressed over it. 'Do not grieve over the unbelievers' is interpreted in this sense as a command, not to be distressed.[22]

A double reproach is addressed to Christians. Referring to Sura 5:77, Ṭabarī decries the excesses of Christians, who go so far as to believe in the divinity of Christ and who call Muḥammad a liar,[23] which is equivalent to rejecting his prophetic office. In another place, this reproach against *takdhīb* is repeated;[24] yes, they are unbelievers who deny what they have recognized as true.[25]

(*b*) The dogmatic theologians of the Ashʿarīya, the branch of Sunni Islam which has been authoritative from the tenth century up to the present, took up these reproaches against Christianity. Al-Bāqillānī (d. AD 1013) in his *Kitāb at-tamhīd* included unbelievers in a kind of programmable statement under the notion 'Ahl al-kufr wa'l-jaḥd wa't-takdhīb'.[28] *Kufr* is, to a certain extent, then, seen as the opposite (*ḍidd*) of belief; it is, so to speak, belief in what is contrary to true belief. 'It is the opposite of belief, ignorance of God; it considers him (Muḥammad) a liar and conceals knowledge of him from the heart of man.[27] Islam, the obedient acceptance of the will of God, would be the proper stance of faith pleasing to God'. Unbelief, on the other hand, means *takdhīb*,[28] denial (*jaḥd*) and disavowal (*inkār*).[29]

We can appreciate, therefore, why Muslim dogmatic theologians in general lay such a heavy emphasis on establishing the trustworthiness and sincerity of the Prophet. If they succeed in this, then the content of the Koran is also incontestably established. It is remarkable, in this connexion, that *takdhīb* is mentioned as a criterion for refusing the Prophet's message. Hence the question of the truth of the Koranic revelation is fused with the question of the intention and moral integrity of the Prophet. Muslim dogmatic theologians sincerely try to prove that Muḥammad speaks the truth (*ṣaddaqa*), and in this way challenge the assertion that Muḥammad was a liar. Everything depends upon the way this question is resolved. It is within this context as well that the miracles of the Prophet (*muᶜjizāt*) are to be understood.[30]

The Muslim position, to my knowledge, has not changed substantially, even in recent times. Efforts at Muslim renewal and dialogue with Christianity, as we find them, for example, in Muḥammad ᶜAbduh and others, do not even take up the truth question. Muḥammad ᶜAbduh sought only to prove that the faith of the Muslim fit well the modern age, indeed especially his time (1848–1905), in marked contrast to Christianity.

When the larger comprehensive works, such as the *Mughnī* of the Muᶜtazilite al-Jabbār (d. AD 1025)[32] or the *Kitāb at-tamhīd* of al-Bāqillānī,[33] deal with the topic of Christianity, they limit themselves to reporting the various positions and schools of thought within Christianity in regard to a particular problem. Direct polemic is superfluous in most cases, for the contradictory positions of the various Christian sects speak for themselves. Direct disputation against the New Testament Gospels is the preserve of another group of writers.

(*c*) The best known examples of this form of 'controversy-literature' are the *'Kitāb al-Faṣl fī'l-milal wa'l-ahwā' wa'n-niḥal'* of

Ibn Ḥazm (d. AD 1064), Shahrastānī's (d. AD 1153) work about religious parties and philosophical schools, and 'Al-Ghazālī's Tract Against the Divinity of Jesus',[34] the authenticity of which is disputed. The most comprehensive and knowledgeable work is one which also had a history of particularly strong impact, the *Tuḥfa* of ᶜAbdallāh at-Tarjumān, alias Fray Anselmo Turmeda, a monk who was converted to Islam (d. between AD 1422 and 1430, probably 1425).[35]

Following an established schema, Turmeda begins his attack against Christianity with the charge of forgery (*taḥrīf*).[36] He alleges that the evangelists, with the exception of John, did not know Jesus personally, and therefore that Matthew, Mark and Luke cannot be considered as authentic witnesses. The extent to which the evangelists 'lie' (*kadhaba*) is shown in Matthew when he says that Jesus remained three days and three nights in the grave, just as Jonah spent the same amount of time in the belly of the fish. If one calculates exactly, however, Jesus lay in the tomb only one day and two nights.[37] Turmeda gives special attention to the problems of Incarnation[38] and Trinity.[39] Above all, the miracles of Jesus appear to the former Christian theologian absolutely insufficient proofs of the divinity of Jesus.[40] His comparison of the Synoptic Gospels strikes one as remarkably modern.[41] He points out, for example, that John, the only evangelist who knew Jesus, reports nothing about the institution of the Eucharist.[42] It is remarkable that in his polemic against baptism,[43] the Eucharist[44] and the sacrament of penance,[45] Turmeda makes a number of highly interesting observations concerning details of liturgical history, of which de Epalza offers explanations in his Spanish translation and critical edition. Turmeda concludes his *Tuḥfa* with a discussion of Muḥammad's prophetic office[46] and with his famous Paraclete chapter,[47] according to which the biblical expectation of the Paraclete was fulfilled in the person of the Prophet Muḥammad. As is well-known, this Paraclete-theme determined the lines of Muslim-Christian argumentation for centuries, both before and after Turmeda.

We turn now from Turmeda to the modern era, of which '*Ma ᶜa l-masīḥ fī l-anājīl al-arbaᶜa'* by Fatḥī ᶜUthmān[48] is the most significant representative. The author eagerly compiles western positions which in his opinion seem to support the thesis of the forgery of Scripture. Regretably, he appears to have been unaware of the work of modern Christian exegesis. Muslims who are well versed in modern Christian theology, particularly exegesis, are indispensable for the progress of any Muslim-Christian dialogue. Such an expertise would spare Muslims the painstaking investigation of New Testament texts carried out in the spirit of controversy-literature whose results have usually already been anticipated by modern New Testament exegesis and, by and large, accepted by the official theology of the Christian churches. In any case, on the basis of such results Muslims will ask Christians: Is not the change of content of the proclamation, that is, the transition from the Jesus who preached to the Jesus who is preached, a falsification of the proclamation?

We have seen that Islam frequently associates Christians with unbelievers. It is also clear that Islam's understanding of its relation to unbelievers as, in a sense, a relation to polytheists has nothing to do with the substantial issues of future Muslim-Christian dialogue. Attention must rather be turned to the particular nature of Islam's relation to Christianity. As people of the book, Christians are non-Muslims and, therefore, according to Koranic usage, 'unbelievers'. Nonetheless, Christians are remarkably close to the '*ahl at-tauḥīd*', the Muslims, from a theological perspective. This close relationship is, however, one-sided. It is recognized by the Muslims, but not by Christians. This fact must be recognized and taken into account in future Muslim-Christian dialogue.

Notes

1. Cf. e.g., Sura 27:40.
2. *Encyclopedia of Islam*, new edition I (1960 ff.), s.c. Ahl al-kitāb (G. Vajda), pp. 264–6.
3. It should be noted that the Muslim notion of revelation is different from that of Judaism and Christianity. See L. Gardet & M. Anawati, *Introduction à la*

théologie musulmane. Essai de théologie comparée (Paris, 1948), pp. 392 f., 407–15.

4. J. van Ess, 'Islam', in: E. Brunner-Traut, *Die fünf grossen Weltreligionen* (Freiburg i. Br., 1974), p. 68.
5. Compare *Encyclopedia of Islam,* New edition IV, 'kāfir' (W. Björkman).
6. Sura 98:6–8.
7. Cf. G. E. von Grunebaum, *Der Islam im Mittelalter* (Zürich & Stuttgart, 1963), p. 192, Discussions inside Islam became so sharp that considerations for the justification of *jihād* by the Sunnis against Safavid Persia were proposed, cf. Faḍl-allāh ibn Rūzbihān Khūnjī, *Kitāb-i sulūk al-mulūk* (Hyderabad, Deccan 1386, h/1966), pp. 451 ff.
8. Ibn Manẓur, *Lisān al- arab*, V (Beirut, 1957), p. 144.
9. R. Paret, 'Toleranz und Intoleranz im Islam', in: *Saeculum*, 21 (1970), pp. 344–65; *idem., Mohammad und der Koran* (Stuttgart, 2nd. ed., 1966), pp. 92 ff.
10. For this set of issues, see A. Fattal, *Le statut des non-Musulmans en pays d'Islam* (Beirut, 1958).
11. R. Paret, *Toleranz ...*, pp. 363 f.
12. Likewise they did not produce any easily interpretable summas, similar to those of the scholastic theologians of the Middle Ages. Concerning the problematics of dogmatic theology in Islam cf. Peter Antes, *Prophetenwunder in der Aš ᶜariya bis al-Gazālī* (Algazel) (Freiburg i. Br., 1970), p. 9–20.
13. The Koranic verses are Sura 2:105; 3:64, 110–113; 199; 5:15–19, 44–52, 59, 65–68, 77; 29:46; 98:1, 6. The commentaries refer to the People of the Book and unbelievers also in connexion with a number of other verses. For example, see the interpretation of Sura 2:6–9 in Ibn ᶜArabī, *Tafsīr al qur'ān al-karīm*, Vol. I (Beirut, 1387 h/1968), pp. 19 f.
14. Tafsīr at-Ṭabarī, *Jāmi ᶜal-bayān ᶜan ta'wīl al-qur'ān*, 16 vols (Cairo, 1346 h/1927–8), Vol. 2. p. 470 (from now on quoted as Ṭabarī).
15. Cf. *Encyclopedia of Islam*, IV (1934), s.v. 'shirk' (W. Björkman).
16. Ṭabarī VII, p. 105. A third sin is mentioned here, namely to do what God has forbidden. This sin, however, is not significant in our context.
17. Ṭabarī VII, p. 107. In pp. 118 ff, in his discussion of verse 113, Ṭabarī points out that the *ahl al-kitāb* is not a uniform grouping. On the basis of Sura 2:110, among the *ahl al-kitāb* there are both believers and unbelievers. Others, however, relate the difference to the comparison of the *ahl al-kitāb* with the *umma* of the prophet Muḥammad.
18. Ṭabarī VII, p. 496–501.
19. Ṭabarī X, p. 146.
20. Ṭabarī X, pp. 146 f.
21. Ṭabarī X, pp. 373 f.

22. Ṭabarī X, p. 475 contains the commentary on Sura 5:68.
23. Ṭabarī X, pp. 487 f.
24. Ṭabarī, *Tafsīr al-qur'ān*, part 30 (Cairo, 1329 h/1911), p. 169.
25. Ṭabarī, *Tafsīr al-qur'ān*, part 21 (Cairo, 1328 h/1910), p. 4.
26. al-Bāqillānī, *Kitāb at-tamhīd* (Beirut, 1957), No. 621.
27. Id., No. 583. According to Sura 59:16, the devil is responsible for unbelief. For a discussion of the devil and his rôle in evil, see P. Antes, 'The First Aš[c]arites' Conception of Evil and the Devil', in: *Mélanges offerts à Henry Corbin*, ed. S. H. Nasr (Teheran, 1977), pp. 177–89. The context suggests that the personal pronoun refers back to God. The critical apparatus, however, allows of the possibility that there is an unintentional reference to Muḥammad, although neither his name nor the formula of blessing for him appear in the text, since one manuscript elucidates the issue by speaking of knowledge about 'God' (rather than 'him').
28. See also al-Baghdādī, *Uṣūl ad-dīn* (Istanbul, 1346/1928), p. 248.
29. al-Bāqillānī, *op. cit.*, No. 583.
30. Cf. P. Antes, *Prophetenwunder*, pp. 29 ff.
31. Muhammad [c]Abduh, *Risālat at-tauḥīd* (Cairo, 12th ed. 1366/1946), Engl. transl. by I. Musā[c]ad & Kenneth Cragg: *The Theology of Unity* (London, 1966); M. [c]Abduh, *al- Islām wa' n-naṣrāniyya ma[c]a'l-[c]ilm wa'l-madaniyya* (Cairo, 3rd. ed., 1341/1921), German translation by G. Hasselblatt, in his thesis: *Herkunft und Auswirkungen der Apologetik Muhammad [c]Abduhs (1849–1905), untersucht an seiner Schrift: Islam und Christentum im Verhältnis zu Wissenschaft und Zivilisation* (Göttingen, 1968). Discussion with Christianity is the topic mainly of the second work cited. On pp. 227 ff. Hasselblatt additionally deals with Taufīq Ṣidqī, al-[c]Aqqād, Sḥāhāta und Shalṭūṭ. For issues relevant to the contemporary Muslim-Christian dialogue, see Y. Moubarac (ed.) *Les Musulmans. Consultation islamo-chrétienne* (Paris, 1971).
32. Cf. G. Monnot, *Penseurs musulman et religions iraniennes, 'Abd al-Jabbār et ses Devanciers* (Paris, 1974). The discussions with Christianity are found in *Mughnī*, V pp. 81–151. There the various positions of the Christian schools of thought are summarized. Cf. also T. Baarda, 'Het ontstaan van de vier Evangelien volgense [c]Abd al-Djabbār., in: *Nederlands Theologisch Tijdschrift*, 28 (1974), pp. 215–38.
33. al-Bāqillanī, *op. cit.* Nos. 132 ff.
34. Title of the German translation by F. E. Wilms: *al-Ghazalīs Schrift wider die Gottheit Jesu* (Leiden, 1966); cf. also R. Parent, *Toleranz . . .*, pp. 362 f. Al-Ghazzālī died in AD 1111.
35. M. de Epalza, *La tuḥfa, autobiografia y polémica islamica contre el Cristianismo de Abdallāh al-Tarǰumān* (fray Anselmo Turmeda) (=Atti

della Academia Nazionale die Lincei, Rome 1971) (quoted as Epalza). For the history of its impact see pp. 43 ff.

36. *Shorter Encyclopedia of Islam*, ed. A. J. Wensinck & J. H. Kramers (Leiden, 1941), s.v. 'taḥrīf' (F. Buhl).
37. Epalza, pp. 293 f.
38. *id.*, pp. 299, 327 335 ff, 383 ff.
39. *id.*, pp. 319 ff, 369 ff.
40. *id.*, pp. 343 ff., 437 f.
41. *id.*, pp. 273 ff, 405 ff, 431 ff.
42. *id.*, p. 451.
43. *id.*, pp. 311 ff.
44. *id.*, pp. 349 ff.
45. *id.*, pp. 361 ff.
46. *id.*, pp. 471 ff.
47. *id.*, pp. 481 ff.
48. ᶜUthman's book appeared in 1966 in Cairo. It actually belongs more to modern Muslim literature on Jesus, cf. Schumann, *Der Christus des Muslime* (Gütersloh, 1975).

Secularization—A theme in Christianity's Dialogue with Non-Christian Religions

Horst Bürkle

The development which we call 'secularization' was prepared for by the Judaeo-Christian tradition and its wide-scale effects, first upon the Hellenistic-Roman civilization and later upon that of Europe as a whole. In its genesis, secularization is most intimately connected with the Christian religion, but today it presents a challenge and an opportunity for every religion as well.[1]

Increasingly, society conceives of itself as autonomous. An understanding of the world and of man that is totally immanent denies the presuppositions necessary for a religious interpretation of life. Hence the great world religions now enjoy a solidarity they had never known before; it rests on the fact that 'they are all being called into question'.[2]

It is precisely this, however, that has stimulated renewal and enactment of traditions, above all among Asiatic religions.[3] Here are the 'opportunities' which, if they are taken advantage of, can indeed lead to new mass religious movements (for instance, in South America, Africa and Japan).[4] These movements are sometimes referred to as 'new religions'. Such a designation fails to appreciate that the syncretistic character of these movements implies a meaningful revitalization of older religious traditions. Challenged by encounter with the modern world, these religions react to secularization by reform and by an apologetic-missionary interpretation of the core of their tradition.

Christianity has been involved in this commonly observable development in two ways. It provided the intellectual prerequisites which eventually enter the 'secularization process'. At the same time, it offers orientations which are conditions for other religious reforms and reactions to secularization. In this sense, Christianity plays a peculiar dual rôle: on the one hand, it fostered the historical process which at this stage has allowed a society to come into existence which is emancipating itself from its essential basis in God. On the other hand, Christianity remains—because of this, becomes—the favoured point of reference and dialogue partner for other religions. Each rôle involves the other.

This can be shown in the case of the beginnings of the reform of Hinduism in the second half of the nineteenth century. In view of certain religious customs (for example, burning of widows) or social regulations (for instance, the caste system), the question of criteria for a contemporary understanding of their own heritage was posed for Hindus when they encountered the Christian religion and modern western civilization. In place of the community of one's birth, first the new national state and then the whole of mankind become the frame of reference for one's own religion.[5] Hand in hand with this development, came a universalization of the individual's own religious self-understanding, thanks to a growing awareness by more and more people of the 'wide world'. One result of this broadening of vision has been a new type of missionary consciousness and the establishment of missionary bases of operations, primarily in the secularized nations of Europe and North America.[6] A book title such as *Asian Missionary Activity in the West*[7] expresses concisely a new state of affairs in regard to 'secularization'.

In the course of contemporary reforms, we can see aspects and phenomena of religions which had their origins in Judaeo-Christian tradition. I point out only the most important:[8]

1. An historical orientation in place of a mythic-cyclic understanding of time as closed in on itself.
2. The modern man as recipient of a religious message addressed

precisely to him. The religious message orients, helps man to find meaning, and leads him to a fulfilled life in its totality.

3. A new ethic of concern for one's neighbour and of social responsibility.
4. The rise of religious communities in the sense of corporate bodies similar to churches.
5. Revivification of rites, symbols, cultic actions as religious celebrations and disciplines against the background of, and as supplements to, the secularized life style of our time.

In these developments, the Christian tradition and the contemporary churches, either consciously or not, play the rôle of 'silent partners' in dialogue. Dialogue with other religions is of prime interest to Christian theology, given the general phenomenon of secularization. Christianity itself, as a result of the secularization which it fostered, now needs to renew and rediscover its own traditions. The development which in the West led to so-called 'secularism' resulted in a steady process of reduction and loss of the substance of Christianity in the Church. Improper or often one-sided forms in which Christianity has tried to realize itself have tended to lead away from the Christian religion rather than to its heart. Christian religion as a *praxis pietatis* which affects all areas of the individual and community life has shrunk to mere vestiges of what it once was.[9]

Liberation from a heteronomous existence in a mythico-magical world and life in the 'worldly' world of our modern age has been accompanied by, and has resulted in, unexpected and new forms of dependency for secular man; he seems autonomous and has become religionless. Since the 'danger' is common and worldwide, the issue of secularism demands inter-religious discussion. Such a discussion would also afford Christian theologians the opportunity to learn and profit from the insights of the representatives of other religions. They would become aware of what is hidden, or handed on unconsciously, in the history of their Church. Consideration of another religion's efforts at renewal may help to overcome the functional blindness characteristic of one who has severely limited his horizons by looking at nothing outside his own church spire. A Christian concerned with secularism must consider the reactions of various other religions to the same phenomenon.

Here I survey the responses of various religions to secularization. This cannot be an exhaustive examination. The forms of response of the individual religions are too numerous; and the situations and levels of development of peoples and societies in question are too varied. My examples will help others to examine the data by means of a model. With the aid of such a model, I shall attempt to define the essential problems more precisely.

The new forms of life in the secular world do not make older religious ties superfluous. Man's newly acquired technological expertise and his life in an urbanized or industrialized society do not in themselves imply an abolishment of the religion of his fathers. Even African tribal religions, in which the connexion with a particular community and a particular location play a central rôle, have been able to display a new great energy and strength in altered conditions. For instance, on the edges of the rapidly growing African conurbations, and in the workers' settlements of the Republic of South Africa, a reawakening of elements of tribal religion is evident in the various sectarian religious movements. But even without any symbiotic relationship with Christian tradition, older African beliefs and practices live on in their own peculiar ways. It appears that the modern life with all its technological advances that is so much desired by men still leaves men dissatisfied. That is usually most evident when enlightened, planned and organized modern life yields to a kind of 'limit-situation'. In a crisis, a man relies more on the strengths of his ancestral faith than on the assurances and protections of the modern secularized world. Consequently, one can again and again observe in Africa peculiar combinations of secular life and religious practices which try to ensure life and well-being in the fashion of the older paganism.

This combination is observable, for instance, in the case of sickness. Modern Western medical care does not seem to respond to the African's age-old sense of 'total therapy'. Admission to a government hospital and submission to surgical procedures do not rule out subsequent consultation with the witch-doctor. This behaviour manifests an underlying pre-Christian understanding of sickness as something more than physical injury. For the African and his religious consciousness, the roots lie much deeper. They extend into the disturbed context of life and existence. Physical suffering and illness are the visible signs of a condition which, in its origins, needs religious help. The Belgian missionary, Placide Tempels, indicated in his analysis of Bantu thought[10] the important rôle the life-force or life-preserving power (*force vitale*) plays for the African. Through the hierarchy of communities and kinship systems, such vitalizing power is delegated from gods and ancestral spirits to men. When the power is refused or when the carefully balanced system of such power influences is disturbed, life is endangered. The various stages of the individual's life and social relations in a community are determined by this wider context of existence, and take it into account in numerous rites and cultic celebrations.

Medically prescribed remedies and the surgical scalpel cannot penetrate this world of essential relations once it has been disturbed. Therefore, despite modern methods of treatment, man finds that in the areas of his life which cannot be secularized he is dependent upon incantations and magical rites. Consequently, a certain kind of symbiosis can result in which the world of ancestral spirits continues to exercise power over a man who drives a motor car, has X-rays taken, or uses a machine-gun. It is evident from these examples that in an increasingly secularized world religion does not simply disappear but can assert itself in an altered form, even under new conditions. A new system of belief can prevail over the older religion only if it succeeds as completely as the older religion did in reaching into the depths of reality and, thus grounded in reality, can relate to life in a secularized world.

A contemporary educated African's ties to his traditional tribal religion can assume for him the character of the dialectic of 'faith and knowledge'. He does not ignore the critical question: what rôle can traditional ideas and experience play in the context of modern life? Study of their tradition, mainly orally transmitted myths and folktales, study of the value-systems of particular tribal societies and the laws regulating their communal life are among the areas of study and research most favoured by African students. It is not surprising that well-educated 'witch doctors' have been invited to give lectures and attend discussions at universities, as was the case, for example, in Kumasi (Ghana) and Kampala (Uganda). These 'witch doctors' are themselves thoroughly 'modern men'. They conduct a sort of consultation hour in the style of medical practice and are prepared with rational arguments to discuss their procedures. Such examples, although they are doubtless exceptions, indicate that the representatives of the heritage of tribal religions are not willing to capitulate before the questions of critical reason. They are prepared to defend against the objections of modern thought what for them has seemed so obvious for so long.

Efforts at a deeper understanding and intellectual analysis of traditional material are often bound up with a decidedly negative attitude to western ideas and Christian modes of thought. Jomo Kenyatta dedicated his studies in London to the service of the renaissance of the thought of his tribal community, the Gikuyu.[11] The methods of western ethnological research are used to investigate the value systems of Africans which are essential for the building of a new Africa. Africans want to be free of patterns imposed by the West, and to make use of ideals indigenous to their own tribal traditions in building independent African states. Julius Nyerere points therefore to the ancient African ideal of community, the *ujamaa*, as a basis for the 'African Socialism' he has called for: 'We Africans do not need to be "converted" to Socialism any more than we must "learn" democracy. Both have their roots in our own past—in the traditional society from which we have been brought forth'.[12] The ancestral spirits who once served the wider community of the living with the living dead now serves as the foundation for a new political state. What today appears as a timely ideal of unlimited *esprit de corps* is a part of traditional African religion that has been taken over into the present in secular form.

Leopold S. Senghor has attempted the most inclusive synthesis of the African past and modern thought. He has posed most pointedly the question of African identity in the face of a modern world which changes and alienates the African. His programme of *négritude* is, however, no mere attempt to express their own past for Africans. Senghor views the synthesis of traditional African 'wisdom' and a humanism grounded in Christianity as a contribution to the problems of humanity as a whole. Africa has a message for the rest of the world. This message emerges as the inheritance of the African communities and may not be supplanted or 'outstripped' by modern culture. Secularized man is in radical need of such information and orientation. In Senghor's opinion, the African can render this service, precisely because he is more firmly rooted in these values than western man, who has been impoverished by materialism and rationalism. '*Négritude* is, as I like to express it, the totality of the cultural values of the black world, as they are expressed in our life, in our institutions, in our deeds . . . Our main concern was that . . . we accept this *négritude*, that we live it out, and then, after we have existentially experienced it, that we deepen its significance. Finally, we will offer it as a gift to serve as a cornerstone for the establishment of 'universal civilization', which will either be the common enterprise of all races, all civilizations, or else it will not be at all'.[13] Here a synthesis has taken place between the religious heritage of tribal society and the western spirit. It is a synthesis which can no longer be called specifically religious in the narrower sense. Senghor's is the most sophisticated way of viewing the relationship of tradition to the present. It surpasses other forms of synthesis, for instance, that of the modern witch doctor in an African city. Common to all these forms, however, is the fact that decisive solutions to the problems of individuals as well as of society are sought not from the technical advances of the enlightened West, but from the African's own roots, which are fundamentally religious.

Traditional religion is fully capable of providing assurance and support for life in the technological age. That a man makes use of machines does not necessarily imply that he has abandoned the magical beliefs of this ancestors. Margaret Field, an English psychotherapist, has gathered abundant material from Ghana which illustrates how traditional concepts and supports for life can win new significance precisely under modern conditions. For example, she collected and evaluated approximately a hundred and fifty sayings painted on taxis and trucks, as they are found time and again in modern Ghana. 'My car is assured against any accident'. 'Everyone will die'. 'I have seen my end'. 'I have a special protecting spirit, I am protected by the Most High'. Familiarity with and use of a varied technology have not freed man from the need to find a way to protect and insure his life in this revolutionarily new technological world. In his need, he turns to incantations which refer back to the world of traditional securities for life, of bearers of extraordinary power and of his ancestors. The motor car and the aeroplane have not supplanted traditional religion, but have given it a new function in a new situation. In response to a life that has been changed in many respects, the African discovers new relevance in his traditional religious ties. The function of the world of his gods has, in a way, been 'transposed'. At first, the world of his gods was in the midst of his everyday world. Now it is on the edge of this rationalized, technological world, where man experiences crises and therefore the limits of secularization.

What does the fact that traditional African tribal religion has not been suppressed by modern development but rather continues to endure in a sort of 'symbiosis' mean for Christian proclamation? The Christian mission must reckon with the fact that at crisis-points a modern non-Christian will turn to traditional patterns of religious behaviour. While traditional religion has declined, it has also showed signs of its power to endure under altered circumstances. Tribal religion first served to support and assure life. As technology advances, there is less need for religion as a support for day-to-day existence.

When he experiences his life as threatened, or radically limited, man still looks to the help of overbearing representatives of power, such as are accessible to him in traditional tribal religion. It would be shortsighted, therefore, to assume that the advance of western civilization and technological development necessarily prepare the ground for Christian missionary proclamation. The dimension of life to which tribal religions properly refer cannot even be touched by the altered and improved circumstances in which a person finds himself. That is why missionary proclamation must address itself to the deep-rooted loyalties of the African's religious consciousness in order to integrate them in this context. This cannot be done by looking back to the model of an unchanged, thoroughly intact tribal religion. Tribal religion exists in such a state only in rare circumstances. Christian missionary activity has to challenge the traditional religion with the proclamation of the sovereignty of Christ Jesus precisely at the 'limit-situations' of modern existence. Christian missionary activity will try to discover the religion of the African, latent and hidden in the various forms of secular life, because the African religious consciousness knows by an innate understanding that the mystery of life is deeper than the secularized world—which is subject to manipulation—would lead him to believe. As we have seen, a more profound religious perception of tribal belief staunchly protests against the superficial understanding of life which the secular world offers. Proclamation in the name of Jesus Christ has all the more reason to dismantle the utopian expectations for a perfect and therefore religionless world which accompany secularization. In a way that the remaining and still living elements of tribal religion cannot afford, Christianity can witness to the fact that all problems and questions are not resolved as technology and society advance.

Such a witness presumes preparation through a mission theology which considers the recipient of the proclamation in his totality. This totality includes the realm of the subconscious, which is of critical significance, and not only in the case of men of tribal religion. The rational form of the Christian message in teaching and preaching, as it has taken shape in the West, is inadequate in this context. The more the subconscious and irrational dimensions of the person are neglected in the process of secularization, the more open this realm of the person will be to affiliation with other religions. Christian belief that does not reach the levels of the subconscious will produce—not only in Africa and Asia—a superficial Christianity. The number of sects in Africa has an important message for us. The body-soul unity has an important rôle to play in proclamation addressed to the whole man, as is evident in the association of physical with spiritual healing by African witch doctors today.

A third factor which is essential for missionary proclamation touches on the relationship of individual and community. For the African who is grounded in his religion, the community's interests are set before individual interests. In his religion, too, he never understands himself simply as an individual but always as a member of a common unity. When radical social changes isolate him and separate him from his traditional communities, he seeks substitutes for his community. New religious groupings replace his crumbling ancestral community. Christian proclamation must avoid an exclusive concern with the individual and emphasize the corporate character of Christianity, that is, the fact that being a Christian means being a member of the community. An individual's personal decision has as its background the community of believers which, as the Body of Christ, exists prior to every individual conversion.

Religious traditions are discovering their significance for the formation of ethics in an age of secularization. The new secular states of Asia and Africa need citizens who act responsibly. In the quest for an ethical basis for the new civil society, these states return to their own religious traditions. Especially in India, for example, the movement for political independence from a colonial power went hand-in-hand with the movement for the reform of Hinduism. In both cases, India was reacting to prevailing western influences. Liberation from political domination was accompanied by a desire for freedom from spiritual tutelage by the West. India experienced a renaissance—certaily not without the influence of western scholars of Indian religions—of certain elements of its own religious tradition. Individuals can respond to the challenges involved in the growth of a modern secular state by making use of the strengths inherent in the religious tradition of their ancestors.

Renewed Hinduism's response to contemporary social responsibility affords a particularly striking example of how a nation can use its religious heritage. An irrevocable challenge for civil society became the occasion for a deeper understanding of a religious tradition. The ahistorical, eternal succession of becoming and of passing away, as well as the never-ending cycle of individual rebirth, corresponded to an attitude of flight from the world. Salvation consisted in turning away from the problems of this world, not in solving them. He who was too involved in the lowlands of this world ran the risk, consequently, of losing eternal salvation. The 'great refusal' signified, therefore, a No to a superficial therapy for symptoms which satisfied itself as a response to individual grievances. What was truly important was that man should move beyond this world of illusion and return to unity with his origin. The mystical unification of the individual with the divine *brahma* frees him from all the deficiencies of this life. Since for the Hindu there is no real development and no goal in history, it is not to his advantage to involve himself seriously in this world of eternal recurrence (*samsara*). On the contrary, it was dangerous to interfere in the natural course of things. He who desires to change something risks violating eternal law (*dharma*). With Goethe, we can say that everyone must complete the circuit of his life according to eternal decree. The place assigned to the individual in life is regarded as unchangeable, as sacred necessity. The individual must not attempt to change this situation but accept and endure it as inevitable. No one should rebel against the results of his process of reincarnation. Everyone must accept life as it is and not alter it in any way. Given these presuppositions, it is evident that the caste system in India could not be regarded merely as a social issue. It was part of a religion which guaranteed the *status quo*. The untouchable was left to his destiny, for it was divinely decreed.

The decisive change occurred when what had previously grounded this religious tradition received an opposite interpretation. The great formula for the world-rejecting and world-damaging message of the Upanishads reads, *tat tvam asi*: that is, 'you are that'. This represents the basic confession of Hinduism, which proclaims redemption (*moksha*) in the unity of the part with the whole, of man with the absolute Unique One. Under the influence of Schopenhauer's thought, the German philosopher Paul Deussen transformed this formula of turning away from the world to a formula of turning to the world and of social responsibility: *tat tvam asi* means not only the unity of every individual with the immutable *brahma*, but a basis for authentic human solidarity. I am always my neighbour too. In 1893, Deussen announced to a gathering in Bombay a message that he contended surpassed that of Christianity. The Sermon on the Mount demands love of one's neighbour; but it does not say how such a love is to be attained. The ancient Indian *tat tvam asi* tradition, on the other hand, makes possible what the Sermon on the Mount requires. From this point, Reform Hinduism has claimed to offer the presuppositions of a socially-responsible ethic. Traditional religious belief is not simply abandoned in the face of the new realities of state and society but is being reinterpreted to make it relevant now.

Something similar occurred in regard to the caste question. Caste belongs essentially to the sphere of religion. Hence it has not been vulnerable to the attacks of the modern democratic point of view. Again, it is part of an ancient doctrine of *dharma*, in which an unchangeable place in the caste system is allotted to each individual. The place of birth and one's family bind the individual religiously. But Hinduism, which created and sanctioned the castes, is used to support opposition against the social injustice of the caste system. Gandhi believed that the untouchables were God's specially favoured children (*harijan*). They enjoyed his special concern, and he defended them to such a degree that if he had the choice, he would be reincarnated as an untouchable. The modern development towards a democratic society does not render the traditional religious system of Hinduism untenable, but mellows its problematics by reference to the supreme love of the Creator for his creatures: 'If God dwells in everything that exists in the universe, that is, if the Brahman as well as the Banghi, the scholar as well as the street sweeper, the Ezhava as well as the Pariah, regardless of the caste to which they belong—if these are from God, there is none who is inferior, all are without exception equal, for they are creatures of that Creator'.[16] For the representatives of the reform of Hinduism, a religion of divinely-sanctioned discrimination has become a religion of new responsibility for one's neighbour.

If we inquire into the motives that were strong enough to effect such a radical transformation, two aspects seem especially important. In constructing a democratic society as a basis for the new national state, the caste system appeared to be an obstacle on the way to the unity of the nation. The question arose of how the religious principles and the whole conceptual context in which the caste system originally had its origins were to be interpreted? The reformers of Hinduism answered this problem by proposing a spiritualized and deepened understanding of the caste system. The claim of the Brahmans to be the religious and intellectual leaders of the people is now no longer conceived of as a privilege of birth. For Radhakrishnan,[17] the true Brahman distinguishes himself by superior character-traits, by goodness of heart and by exemplary ethical conduct. This is not a question of better human intentions and effort, but of something intimately connected with the Hindu notion of religious self-realization. The solution to the problem of true *humanitas* lies once again in man's religion. My example clearly shows that radical changes in the structures of society which were originally supported by religious traditions and principles need not result in a purely secular, religionless situation. In this connexion, we may not overlook the fact that under new civic conditions western ideals of a democratic and social community have exerted significant influence.

Contemporary Muslim theologians are also struggling to show how Islam can be relevant to the exigencies of the present. Islam is proclaimed as a 'force for peace' with new significance for the conflicts of modern society and for the peaceful co-existence of peoples and nations. In a world threatened by nuclear destruction, it is asked what Islam has to contribute to sustaining peace. The guarantee for the unity of humanity, Islam believes, is to be found in the principle of monotheism, whose special defender Islam feels itself called to be. By virtue of this claim, a certain polemic limitation is maintained in regard to Christianity since, in the Muslim view, Christianity's christological dogma destroys the oneness of God. In this context, however, I am less interested in Islam's unjustified criticism of Christian Trinitarian doctrine than in Islam's attempt to prove itself to be the indispensable basis for worldwide understanding and unity among nations, for which secular societies also strive. 'As a first step towards a settlement in international relations, Islam tries to establish the worldwide brotherhood of man. This brotherhood derives directly from the oneness of God, which is the focal point of all Muslim teaching. It is only the kinship of men to one another that is grounded in God, that makes them brothers.'[18] A political ethic such as this, applied to the secular world, makes use of a new exegesis of Koranic texts:

> And hold fast, all together, by the Rope which God (stretches out), and be not divided among yourselves; and remember with gratitude God's favour on you; for you were enemies, and He joined your hearts in love, so that by His Grace you became brethren, and you were on the brink of the pit of fire, and He saved you from it . . . (Sura 3:103).

This prophetic exhortation, which had originally been directed to fostering the unity of the newly-established Muslim community, is now interpreted and understood with reference to the unity and harmony of the whole of humanity. The same holds true in problems of social progress and the demands for the civil rights for all. Contemporary representatives of Islam apply principles that initially related to circumstances within the Muslim community as religious bases for the progress of humanity in general: 'The concept of the brotherhood of man was emphasized by Islam through the abolishment of all privileges based on race, colour, descent, position, possession, and so on . . .' It would be easy to multiply examples of how contemporary Islam has used its religious heritage in a secular world come of age.

Spurred on by new ethical problems, various religious traditions have discovered their particular significance for the needs of modern men and societies. In the face of secularization, non-Christian religions also see it as their task to be guardians of progress. They outspokenly insist on the right use of reason and on the rôle of scientific research. In this regard also, we observe a change in self-understanding among the modern representatives of non-Christian religions. It was initially precisely these religions which prevented a technological and scientific explanation of the world and the conditions in which life has to be lived. For a follower of tribal religion in Africa, his tradition determined his understanding of reality. He did not have any freedom to deal in an 'objective' fashion with the world he encountered. The 'world' which surrounded him was the realm of gods and ancestral spirits. They either guaranteed or prohibited the natural use of objects. Numerous taboos and prohibitions expressed the barriers to and exploration and use of the environment. In India, reverence for the sacred cow still plays a significant rôle and is given greater weight than any political-economic necessity. Today the ever-expanding, irrepressible openness to a technical-rational approach to life's possibilities forces religiously-conditioned restrictions to give way more and more. Secularization allows man to experience his environment as the field of his own free activity. The environment is subject to human planning and development, but no longer bound to religious taboos and magical interpretations.

In response to this development, the representatives of non-Christian religions have also redescribed the rôle of inquiry and critical reason. Religion should be able to free man inwardly to use his gift of reason. Radhakrishnan believes that man is by his nature prejudiced and superstitious. Now it is claimed that it is religious experience alone, as the experience of harmony with universal cosmic being, which provides man with the capacity to relate to the reality of this world in a forthright and authentic way. Scientific research and religious belief are in a mutually enriching relationship. Religion must, therefore, also learn from science: 'The scientific drive for knowledge, with its inexhaustable intellectual questioning, its refusal to take anything merely on faith, and its capacity for critical doubt, is always a stimulus for adventure and experiment'.[19] Hence, research and science can serve as an example for religion in its task of self-reform. Man should also strive in his religion for advance and further development and reject dogmatic perfectionism. This corresponds to modern Hinduism's concept of a universal religion which develops out of and beyond all the traditional distinctions of the various individual religions. This idea itself however is based on the ancient Indian notion of unity in diversity. Here all concrete professions of faith lose their contours. A name becomes mere noise and smoke. The true seer already acknowledges the relativity of all the historically conditioned differences. He therefore refuses to commit himself. Confession and religious affiliation are reduced to mere representations of belief. This is the decisive objection made by modern Hindu thinkers with which Christianity must reckon and which it must answer.

Muslim reforms today demand a free interpretation of the Koran which is no longer bound to the traditional consensus (*ijmāᶜ*). The demand that the Scripture alone should be the normative means, according to Muḥammad ᶜAbduh, that every theologian has the right to unrestricted study of the sources. An exegesis of the Koran related to a particular standpoint will therefore become possible. Such an exegesis will be able to give the text a new relevance. The meaning of a text is determined by the 'pre-understanding' of the interpreter. The decisive question is, therefore, no longer how a Koranic text was interpreted in the past, but what relevance it can have to a modern secular situation.

In view of the special rôle of science and research today, Muslim reforms call to mind Islam's traditional interest in and enthusiasm for the questions of natural science and logic. Modern questions of natural science are already dealt with in the Koran in bold allegorical interpretation. These are questions, for instance, of atomic physics. In an applied sense, one can speak of 'demythologization'. Muslim belief, it is demanded, should follow 'the natural order of things'. It has no need, therefore, for belief in extraordinary or miraculous events. When a literal understanding of a text conflicts with reason, then reason is to prevail. According to Muḥammad ᶜAbduh, religion is 'the friend of science; it stimulates it to investigate the data of the universe. It demands that man should act according to the laws of nature. To do so requires strength of character and readiness for action'.[20] Islam is presented as the 'ideal religion' which is particularly able to do justice to the needs of present-day man. A characteristic of such an ideal religion is the unity of exact knowledge and existential experience. Religious feeling should not merely have a place alongside a practical life dictated by reason. Islamic faith is the central focus by which a person can guide himself in reasonable life. The doctrine of the *Khalīfa*, of the vicegerency of man in the name of Allah (Sura 2:30–33), has a new meaning in the sense of a universal responsibility for man. Allah has assigned to men the responsibility for care and protection of this world. This function entrusted to man (*amānat*) distinguishes him and constitutes his dignity. What heaven and earth refused, man has accepted in belief in God (Sura 33:72): to govern and protect the world according to Allah's mandate.

In viewing this development in the non-Christian religions, the Christian message will turn all the more decisively to those who are fascinated by the possibilities of our science-oriented, technological age. Two aspects are important: Christianity has to point out the inner connexion between the proper use of reason and the *libertas Christiana*, which depends upon the critical use of reason. What is at issue is not merely the historical connexions and the fact that technological advance and scientific research experienced their full opportunity for development within the context of the Christian tradition of the West. Dialogue with other religions on modern man's secular existence must go much deeper. In the mystery of the incarnation we have the foundation for refusing the world any divine attributes. Precisely in God's entering into this world and dealing with it historically in the Son, the world receives its character as 'world'. This character is the presupposition for every scientific approach to the world. In this sense, Friedrich Gogarten interpreted the 'secularizing' of the world as the fruit of a Christian understanding of the world. It is, therefore, a necessary and welcome process which is to be distinguished from 'secularization', which is the autonomy of a man who is no longer conscious that his capacity to participate in worldly existence has come from God. Here missionary proclamation must consider associations which are of pressing importance for men in countries of rapid technical change. The surprising answers which are formulated and offered in the name of non-Christian religions in this context must be examined to see if they are in any way justified, considering the religious tradition in question. Here new points of reference emerge for a missionary proclamation which is prepared for dialogue and no longer orients its message only to the systems of the non-Christian religions, but to the secular reference of those religions.

The second task for Christian theology in this context has to do with the growing secular expectations of non-Christians. The speed and directness with which technical achievements and the advance of civilization have affected Africans and Asians often give rise to utopian expectations. In many cases a political ideology arises which awakens hopes in quasi-eschatological manner. Religions offer themselves, in view of this development, as a help to a sort of 'faith-filled realism'. Here, too, one must examine what presuppositions religions bring to this task. The Church in Asia and Africa has all the more reason to make its message relevant in this respect. Bound up with the Church's service of providing men freedom for dealing with the secular world in a worldly fashion is its responsibility to protect men against utopian misunderstandings of their new world. By referring to the Christ-event, scientific advances and social progress once again relate more realistically to reality. They have no need to become an ersatz religion. In this way, that form of secularism will be confronted 'in which the daring lack of knowledge of the world and its historical relevance is not to be endured, but according to which one presumes to be able to realize the world in its totality' (F. Gogarten).

Repeatedly, we encounter evidence of the fact that non-Christian religions discover their particular function in helping men to understand their true destiny. In the face of secularization's ambivalent character, religion proclaims its proper office. Human reason should be restricted to its limits. Religions speak of the destiny of men, which has its origin in the divine. They speak of the goal of history and challenge men to act in a way relevant to their responsibility for the fate of humanity as a whole. They have replaced a hope for individual salvation with an inclusive view of world and cosmic history.

Such a view corresponds to a new demand which they never felt before, in response to which they direct their missionary efforts to 'all'. They proclaim a message for humanity. However, the message of Jesus as the Christ should not be conceived of in a more restricted sense. When the message of Jesus refers exclusively to the salvation of the individual, it falls short of the renewed religions' proclamation claiming universal significance. The Christian missionary proclamation must take up the universal, indeed cosmic, interpretation of the Lordship of Christ, as already provided in the New Testament. The comprehensive vision of the reality of Christ, as it has found expression in Johannine Logos theology and in the cosmic Christology of the Epistles to the Colossians and Ephesians is of particular significance. Indian Christian theologians remind us today that the personal relationship of the individual to Christ must always be seen within the context of the Lordship of Jesus Christ over all reality.

The testimony of the renewed religions to secularized men is always a testimony to the wholeness of man, to the entirety of man. Religions such as Buddhism and Hinduism present themselves precisely as 'therapeutic' for the man who in secularism has lost touch with his transcendent horizon. Mysticism, yoga, prayer and asceticism appear as ways along which man must proceed if he is to overcome a one-sidedly rationalized, enlightened image of man. We also encounter protest in the renaissance of particular elements of the traditional tribal religions of Africa against a too one-sided, rational image of man. The numerous sectarian movements in Africa are distinguished from the western form of Christianity not least of all in that they address themselves to classes of men who have been neglected in the life and practice of the western-style mission Churches. In the person of the sect's leader, I detect a criticism of a one-sided understanding of the ministerial office, particularly as it has emerged in the Churches of the Reformation.

With his charismatic and prophetic functions, the sectarian leader, not unlike the head of a tribe, determines the whole life of the community. He is not only a preacher who interprets and teaches the Bible, but he carries on the rich cultic traditions of the African religions in liturgical celebration in which, besides the spoken word, the whole community can participate in ritual actions, dance and gesture. The monologue of the officiating pastor is not without disadvantages, even for a congregation of Europeans well-schooled in this sort of worship. For African Christians, pronouncement and communication take place on a much broader base. The means which they employ are more elemental and more direct. Here we encounter the second form of reaction against a Christianity preserved in western forms which occurs not only when it is confronted by African tribal religions. It has reference to the deep levels of the subconscious which can be reached through the language of symbols. Jung's investigation of archetypes has a profound significance for Christianity's proclamation of the reality of Christ to men. In a secular situation in which the imagination and fantasy of man are kept busy by advertising and propaganda, faith—in so far as it wishes to avoid atrophying into a 'world-view'—must not limit itself to purely rational communication and proclamation. It is noteworthy that in the face of the secularization of many areas of life, the religious expression of the African and Asian will definitely not relinquish the use of symbols and ritual.

If the response to the challenge of secularization is to be more than a mere interiorizing of belief, the world must continue to remain open to the experience of the Holy. That means that man's horizons, which narrow themselves more and more in the process of secularization, once again have to open outwards. This is done not by rational concepts alone; it has to make use of the language of symbols and the ritual actions grounded in, and aimed at, an awareness of the Transcendent.

The relationship of the individual to the community is a further example of how religion refers to the whole man. The move from the village into the modern large city means isolation and separation for the African. Instead of fitting in as a member of a community in which he lived and which was also his religious community, he now finds himself in temporary groupings which are purely utilitarian: the workers' quarters, the neighbourhoods of the new dwelling place, the political party, or contacts at his place of work. An African reacts to this situation, which has been familiar to the European for a long time, with a basic need for a community of life and faith. The rapid growth of independent churches and religious groups among people in such a situation has its roots not least of all in the individual's search for a sheltering community. In view of the growing 'loneliness' in secularized society, the Pauline definition of the Christian community as *corpus mysticum* takes on a new significance. The Christian missionary must particularly take into consideration the African's religiously grounded notion of community and must not conceive of the church merely as a congregation who sit and listen to preaching. The dead belong, for the African, to the community of the living. Past has not become mute, as is typical of the bleak view of life of modern man. Man in Africa and Asia is not aware of the feeling that everything starts just now. He experiences life in a continuity which in many respects takes the historical nature of existence more into account than does the unhistorical, atomistic view of the contemporary analysis of existence. The Church as the body of the risen Christ, which by including generations past and to come transcends its visible shape, gains new significance in view of developments outside Europe. It is not many individuals which constitute the community but the mystery of the risen Jesus Christ in corporeal-historical form. All sociological and structural reflections on ecclesiology need to keep in mind this view of the Church which is grounded in its mystery and its continued life and experience.

Christian theology must face the question of how dialogue with non-Christian religions can best be carried out in the service of the emerging Church of Asia and Africa. For a long time, we have maintained an understanding of the Church and of its community which is familiar to us from Western church history. Certain non-European, pre-Christian religious experiences, cultural values and thought-structures will make an important contribution to the

Christians of Asia and Africa who, in the face of movements for independence in their own countries, seek today for their own unique expression of faith and for a new structure for the Church. Secularization in Asia and Africa is accompanied not merely by religious atrophy but has permitted the significance of certain religious traditions and concepts to appear in a new and relevant light. In such instances, secularization actually encourages the emergence of a new religious consciousness.

Notes

1. D. S. Sarma, *Studies in the Renaissance of Hinduism* (Benares, 1944); E. Benz, *Buddhas Wiederkehr und die Zukunft Asiens* (Munich, 1963); R. Paret (ed.) *Die Welt des Islams und die Gegenwart* (Stuttgart, 1961).
2. St C. Neill, 'Sind die Religionen gefährdet?' in: R. Italiaander (ed.) *Die Gefährdung der Religionen* (Kassel, 1966), pp. 11–33.
3. Cf. H. Bürkle, 'Die veränderten Religionen—eine Frage an die Theologie', in: *Radius*, H.3 (1962). pp. 45 ff; *idem*; 'Der Neuhinduismus', in: *Lutherisches Missionsjahrbuch* (1966), pp. 35–51; *idem*; 'Religionen im Dienste der Gesellschaft', in: U. Derbolowsky & E. Stephan (eds.), *Die Wirklichkeit und das Böse* (Hamburg, 1970), pp. 199–208; *idem*; 'Heilsvorstellungen und Heilserwartungen in Asien', in: *Evangelische Theologie*, H.3 (1973), pp. 293–305; *idem.*, 'Die Erneuerung des Menschen in der Sicht des Hinduismus', in: *Studia Instituti Missiologici Societatis Verbi Divini*, No. 13 (1974), pp. 1–13; *idem.*, 'Hindus entdecken den Nächsten', in: P. Rohner (ed.) *Mitmenschlichkeit—eine Illusion?* (Munich, 1973), pp. 101–18. Important parts of this lecture have been published in H. Bürkle, *Die Reaktion der Religionen auf die Säkularisierung* (Neuendettelsau, 1969).
4. Cf. V. Lanternari, 'Religiöse Freiheitsbewegungen unterdrückter Völker', in: *Soziologische Texte*, Vol. 33 (Berlin, 1968), pp. 272–306; E. Fülling, 'Synkretistische Neureligionen in Brasilien', in: E. Dammann (ed.), *Weltmission heute*, H.37/38 (1968), pp. 20–39; B. Sundkler, *Bantupropheten in Südafrika* (Stuttgart, 1964); W. Kohler, *Die Lotus-Lehre und die modernen Religionen in Japan* (Zürich, 1962).
5. 'In this period of creative birth pangs, on account of the depths of its suffering, India has the privilege of being a light for the world, the bearer of a mission of universal significance ... As the typical religion of India, Hinduism represents the spirit whose extraordinary vitality has survived a

variety of political and social changes. As long as there has been a written history, Hinduism has given witness to the sacred flame of the spirit, which must glow forever, even when dynasties fall and empires lie in ruins. The flame of the spirit alone is able to give a soul to our culture and to give men and women a guiding principle by which to live' (S. Radhakrishnan, *Religion und Gesellschaft*, Darmstadt, 1953, p. 47). Examples of religious motivation in the movement for independence can be found in Mahatma Gandhi (cf. H. Bürkle, *Die religiösen Grundlagen im Werk Mahatma Gandhis*) (Darmstadt, 1969).

6. Cf. G. Vicedom, *Die Mission der Welt-Religionen* (Munich, 1959); F. Melzer, *Indien greift nach uns* (Stuttgart, 1962).
7. K. Hutten & S. von Kortzfleisch (eds.), *Asien missioniert im Abendland* (Stuttgart, 1962).
8. We do not consider Islam here; as a post-Jewish, post-Christian religion, in this respect it is to be seen together with both those religions.
9. One such example is the weekly one-hour church service which is supposed to be the 'central event' of the community's week. The kernel of the service in the West is a rationally precise sermon, which, in the majority of cases reaches only a small percentage of the members of the community (cf. E. Stammler, *Protestanten ohne Kirche*, Hamburg, 1967).
10. P. Tempels, *Bantu-Philosophie* (Heidelberg, 1956).
11. J. Kenyatta, *Facing Mount Kenya. The Tribal Life of the Gikuyu* (London, 1965).
12. J. Nyerere, *Freedom and Unity* (Dar es Salaam, 2nd ed., 1967).
13. L. S. Senghor, *Négritude et humanisme* (Paris, 1965) p. 9.
14. M. Field, *Search for Security. An ethno-psychiatric study of Rural Ghana* (London, 1960).
15. P. Hacker, 'Schopenhauer und die Ethik des Hinduismus', in: *Saeculum* XII 4, pp. 366–399.
16. M. K. Gandhi, in 'Harijan' of 30.1.1937.
17. S. Radhakrishnan, *Die Gemeinschaft des Geistes. Östliche Religionen und westliches Denken* (Baden-Baden, 2nd ed., 1961) p. 374.
18. Zafrulla Khan, *Der Islam und die internationalen Beziehungen* (Hamburg, 1958), p. 3.
19. S. Radhakrishnan, *Erneuerung des Glaubens aus dem Geist* (Frankfurt a.M., 1959), p. 18.
20. Cited in D. M. Donaldson, *Studies in Muslim Ethics* (London, 1963), p. 251.

Mystical Dimensions of Islamic Monotheism

Richard Gramlich

Islam is a strictly monotheistic religion. Preserving faith intact means above all preserving monotheism intact, and therefore the rejection of every polytheism. Hence the basic credal formula of Islam at least in its wording, is negative, a rejection. It does not intend to say directly what is, but what is not: 'I testify: There is no god but God'.

The fact that Islam from the start encounters us somewhat defensively postured, shows its deepest concern: the preservation of absolute monotheism. Monotheism is the soul of Islam. In the following pages I shall say something about how the welfare of this soul was attended to in Islam. I leave out of consideration zealous heresy-hunting and theological sophistry offered in the interest of monotheism. I am concerned only with the consequences which Muslim piety, particularly in its mystical forms, has drawn from Islam's fundamental monotheistic posture.

Schematizing and simplifying somewhat phenomena which are quite complex, I arrange the major ideas under three aspects:

1. God as He who alone is goal;
2. God as He who alone acts;
3. God as He who alone has being.

1. *God as He who alone is goal*

According to orthodox Islam, the confession of the tongue and the conviction of the heart constitute faith. In addition, works are required either as an essential component of faith, or as a complement to it. The external act is not so important for the individual pious Muslim as the interior attitude: his pure intention, his sincerity. His motto is: 'An action which is religious becomes religious by means of sincerity'.[1] An action is only sincere when it is an expression of monotheistic faith. That occurs only when God is the sole goal of the act, when the intention of the act is directed solely to God.[2] He who has other goals is a practical polytheist; according to a favourite expression, he practices secret polytheism. In this sense, 'everything that one strives for, one worships'.[3] Desire,[4] or soul[5] as the principle of desire, are the false gods. 'When your desire has more power over you than God's command, so that you obey it more than you do God, then you have chosen it to be your god, and you address to it the *Allāhu Akbar*'.[6]

There is a related attitude, which can be characterized by the motto 'God alone suffices'. 'If a man is totally and completely centred in God, God gives him as His first gift, to be satisfied in God alone'.[7] True knowledge is therefore, to want only one thing in both worlds';[8] the best servant of God is he who 'sees only one, has confidence only in Him, desires Him alone'.[9] The reasonable man does not pursue God's gifts, but God himself.[10] God's friend desires from God nothing but God himself.[11] Expressed metaphorically: 'To think of my Lord is my food, His praise my clothing, shame before Him, my drink'. Once Bāyazīd made a man who wanted to be his disciple fast. On the second day, the man asked for something to eat. Bāyazīd instructed him: 'For us God is nourishment!' The man responded: 'Master, what must be, must be!' Bāyazīd: ' God must be!' The man: 'Master, I only want something that will provide sustenance to enable my body to respond in obedience to God'. Bāyazīd: 'Young man! Bodies have their sustenance in God alone'.[13]

Practical monotheism usually goes hand-in-hand with a visual monotheism, with the spirit's vision of God alone. The admonition to look to the Giver rather than to the gifts belongs to this context. Or man 'sees that the objects are many, he sees that despite their multiplicity, they are proceeding from the One, the Almighty'.[14] The saying: 'I see nothing in which I do not see God', has been ascribed to many great figures in Islam.[15] 'Pure monotheism consists in this, that in all things man sees only God'.[16] The adage 'see God in all things' is superseded in the mystical reversal: 'see all things in God'. One therefore sees 'everything through Him, not Him through a thing'.[17] One professes: 'Never did my glance fall upon a thing, that I did not see that God is nearer than this'.[18] One recognizes the imperfection of one's contemplation when one sees things before one sees God in them.[19] Similar sayings relate to mystic hearing. From every sound, the mystic hears only the divine reality. To this context belong also the many warnings against indifference and forgetfulness of God, and the admonitions to think of God without ceasing. The Baghdadi mystic Shiblī, who, it is alleged, ate only on Fridays, when he visited his master, since the thought of food never came to his mind during the week,[20] explained that, for the gnostics it would be polytheism to forget God for even a moment.[21] Even thinking of Gabriel and Michael was for him polytheism.[22] He reproached a leather worker for forgetting God between every two stitches, and to a disciple he declared: 'If from one Friday to the next anything except God comes to your mind, then you are forbidden to come to me!'[24] He expressed his attitude poetically in these verses:

> Never are my limbs empty of you—
> they are occupied with carrying (my) passion for you.
> God knows: never runs over my tongue
> anything but mention of you.
> You assumed a form while you were in my eye—
> whether you are present or absent, it sees you!

2. *God as He who alone acts*

It is not only a fundamental mistake for a man to think he is able himself to plan his life and make his own decisions. It is a mistake which is also heresy. It is a denial of absolute monotheism, for there is only one who plans, one who decides. Monotheism, therefore, according to one definition, consists in recognizing that God's power is in things without admixture (of any created power), and that this creation of things is without cure; that His activity is the cause of all things, and that His activity has no cause.[26] Good deeds and sin, belief and unbelief, eternal salvation and eternal damnation are also to be ascribed to God alone. Particularly among the early mystics we find strong advocates of this doctrine. It is said: 'God is to be exalted for the actions of His creatures to anger him. Rather, He looked upon certain men with the eye of wrath before He created them, and after He had brought them forth, He caused them to do the works of those who meet with his wrath, in order to cause them finally to dwell in the place of wrath (in hell). Likewise, He is too great for the actions of his creatures to please him. Rather, He looked upon certain men with the eye of his good pleasure before He created them, and after He had brought them forth, He caused them to do the works of those who meet with his good pleasure, in order to cause them finally to dwell in the place of good pleasure (in paradise)'. The following saying is equally significant: 'It is not belief which leads to God, and unbelief which distances us from God. Rather what plays itself out is what was set in motion in the eternity of the divine command for misery and for beatitude. External unbelief is merely the manifestation (of the reality), not (the) reality (itself). The reality is the divine resolve fixed before the aeons and the times'.[28] The same sheikh said: 'Beatitude and misery, error and fidelity ran their course in eternity because of something unalterable, and irrevocable. In time a trace is made to appear in bodies and figures. No one (of his own power) effects the appearance in any way. Nor does any creature have power over them (over beatitude and misery, and so on), they represent a choice which was made in eternity on the basis of previous knowledge, so that the hands of the prophets, and the tongues of God's friends do not attain them, according to the word of God; 'God does not direct aright those whom he led astray'.[29,30]

With sayings such as these, the mystics involve themselves not in a dogmatic issue, but in a genuinely religious concern. Man must capitulate before the omnipotence of God which directs everything; he must surrender himself to God, and recognize Him as sole master. He who considers himself the subject of his actions, arrogates for himself what belongs to God alone. For, 'you know that God was there for you before you were there for yourself. Just as He planned for you before you were or even anything of your plans beside Him, so also He plans for you, after you come into existence. Therefore be for him, as you were for Him (before you came into being) . . .!'

It follows accordingly that 'he who regards (his) deeds as coming from God, is a monotheist'.[32] He who truly knows God, 'sees himself in the grip of the power (of God) in that the omnipotent rule is carried out in him'.[33] He trusts in God, and behaves toward him 'as a dead man before the corpse-washers'.[34] According to another classic definition, monotheism consists in this, 'that man is a figure before God, in which God's plans are executed', whereby God, 'in that which He will of him, takes his place . . . and he is, as he was, before he was'.[35] The mystic sees God, therefore, as Him who alone acts, and sees himself as that in which God's activity takes its course, while contributing or hindering the whole event just as little as he did before his birth. Consequently, he 'commands himself totally to God, to do what He wills',[36] like a dead man, 'whom one can twist and turn as one wills, without his moving or planning',[37] like a chess-piece,[38] with which God plays an eternal game with himself.[39] As a true monotheist, he acknowledges the oneness and uniqueness of God in that, both in his words and in his deeds, he confesses God as Him who alone acts.

This attitude intends only to be an active recognition of the uniqueness, and the transcending majesty and universal efficacy of God, who is the eternally unchangeable not only in a metaphysical sense, doing so in His being and in His decrees, but He who should be revealed as such in the concrete life of man. According to a formula often quoted in mystical circles, 'God should be to you, as He always was'.[40] Or as it is expressed more fully: 'The quintessence of the matter is that it should be evident to you, that there is no one who acts besides God, and that He who alone created . . . and brought in being all that is, is God, who has no partner in His activity. When that has been made clear to you, you look to Him alone. He is the object of your fear, in Him is your hope, in Him your security, in Him your confidence. For He is who (alone) acts, without anyone else. Everything else serves His purpose, without being able on its own to move so much as an atom from the realms of heaven and earth'.[41]

The monotheistic confession of faith: 'There is no god but God', is recast with a view to processes in creations, especially the actions of man, to read: 'There is no one who acts but God'. It does not follow from this that man does not, or should not, act. He should act, but he should know at the same time that he is not the subject of the action, but rather the place in which the divine action, which he does not cause, but rather receives, is made manifest. Not by accident did the same master who compared the monotheistic attitude stance to that of an inanimate chess-piece, and who defined it in another place as 'something, in which traces are obliterated and sciences disappear',[42] harshly rejected any talk of 'renunciation of activities'. 'The people who talk this way represent the doctrine, that one should neglect activity. In my opinion that is a serious mistake. One who says such things is in a worse way than a thief or an adulterer. Those who know God, receive their deeds from God, and in them, they return to God. Had I a thousand years to life, I would not diminish deeds of piety in the least, unless I were to be prevented from doing them. This is a solid principle according to my knowledge, and is very strong in my understanding'.[43]

3. *God as He who alone has being*

In this section I do not treat the problem of Islam's doctrinal monism. I am concerned with a radical form of existential monotheism, which denies to whoever is not divine the right to recognize his own being. We have already seen: 'Activity is proper to God alone, behind the veils of things, which are the locus for the appearance of the Divine activity'.[44] Man does not plan; God plans for him.[45] As in the case of action and planning, so human existence should disappear. Monotheism is 'the annihilation of the traces of what is human, and the isolation of what is divine'.[46] The temporal cannot exist side by side with the eternal-monotheism is 'the separation of the eternal from the temporal'[47]—a human I cannot exist alongside the divine I. 'Whoever speaks of his own being side by side with God's being, documents his unbelief; whoever speaks of God's being side by side with his own being, testifies to his polytheism'.[48] This attitude is visible in the prayer: 'How much further will this individuality that is between you and me go? I beseach You, blot out my individuality from me, so that You may be my individuality, so that You alone remain, and see nothing else beside You'.[49] The mystic must respond to the question whether there is a greater sin than the fact simply that he is.[50] The following words were put into the mouth of Moses, to whom God spoke from the burning bush: 'You are the one who has always been, and who will be for ever. There is no place for Moses besides You, nor dare he speak, unless You allow him to exist through Your existence, and You characterize him with Your own attributes, so that You are at once the one who addresses, and the one who is addressed'. At this point God is supposed to have answered him: 'No one conveys My word except Me, and no one answers Me except Me. I am the speaker, and the one spoken to, and you are a form, in which the words have their place'.[51]

According to a saying of the Prophet, for the man whom God loves, God can be 'the hearing, with which he hears, and the sight with which he sees'. That can also be regarded as indicating that God, just as He takes the place of men in hearing and seeing, can take their place in being.[52] Men then are 'only in existence through His being for them, in so far as He is for the creatures, not, (however) in the sense that He is for their individual selves, (rather) in a sense, which no one except him knows'.[53] 'God assumes in their place what is theirs'.[54] God takes the place of the creaturely being, which is encountered in normal human experience. The monotheistic confessional formula rises from 'no God but God' beyond 'No one acts but God', to 'No one has being but God'. Monotheism means 'that one looks upon things with the eye of non-existence'.[55]

Formulas which express the identity of the mystic with God—and they abound in Islam—intend to assert not a formal identity between two realities, but the real identity of God with himself. If a man can say that he is 'filled from head to toe with God', this is only so because there is of himself 'nothing but the name'.[56] Whoever can say: 'I am He',[57] 'You are no other than I'[58] or 'when you see me, you see Him'[58]—to mention only a few less frequently cited theopathic locutions—he acknowledges that there is only one I, the divine I, in his monotheistic view of the world. He speaks of God in the first person, and his monotheistic confession takes the form: 'There is no I but me'.[60]

The mystic authors have no difficulty in maintaining that God reveals himself in things, and at the same time denying the existence of things. 'He it is, who in diverse forms and in numerous figures and in changing colours has appeared in immaterial and in material objects. The existent, object and reality—and outside of the being and reality of his nature there exists nothing'.[61] In everyday experience one recognizes one's own existence and the being of objects. On the plane of mystical experience, however, God is the sole reality, the unique Existent; in comparison with Him all the non-divine is as appearance is to being.[62] Being is not ascribed to him who is not divine; he has only one function: to be an image for the reality of God, a place of appearance for the Divine. Everything points to the uniqueness of him, besides whom there is no God.

As we consider once again the monotheistic formula 'There is no God but God', it is evident from the foregoing that the man on whom monotheism has been enjoined as a duty is not capable of responding to its demands. He cannot act, therefore he is also unable to make a profession of faith. He cannot or should not be, so also he cannot or should not be a monotheist. To conduct one self as one who acts, and who has existence would be a transgression; to be a monotheist would be a transgression against mystical monotheism. For there is only one true monotheist: God Himself, and that is clearly recognized by Muslim mystics. They explain:

'No creature partakes in the confession of God's oneness. God alone confesses the oneness of God. Confession of oneness belongs to God alone, and creatures live on it as parasites'.[64] 'The confession of oneness has value in the One, not in the creature who confesses the oneness';[65] or as another expresses it: 'The confession of oneness is in reality the property of Him who is confessed as the One, according to its external form, it is the ornament of him who confesses the oneness'.[66] The following formulation is clear: 'In that man confesses that his Lord is the One, he confirms his I (as having existence and as confessing). But he who confirms his I, is guilty of secret polytheism. God alone is He who confesses Himself as the One through the tongues of the creatures he chooses'.[67]

This same thought is expressed poetically in the following verses:

> No one confesses the One as the One,
> for everyone who confesses Him as the One, denies Him.
> Who ever talks about His attribute 'One', his monotheism
> Is meaningless, for the One has made it void and empty.
> God's word that He is the One, is (*true*) monotheism,
> But whoever qualifies Him by an attribute, his attribute is 'heretic'.

Mystical monotheism, in its last consequence, makes man (and with him everything created) is 'as he was before he was'[69] (a well-known saying, attributed to various authors), and that the One God remains 'as He always was'.[70] Small wonder, then, when a mystic thinks that he ought to ask for forgiveness when he says 'God',[71] for in the world of mystical reality 'no one but God has ever said "God"'.[72] And for the mystic this world alone constitutes truth and reality.

Notes

1. Jullābi, Abū'l-Ḥasan ᶜAlī b. ᶜUthmān ibn abī ᶜAlī al-Hujwīrī, *Kashf ul-mahjūb*, Photomechanical reproduction of the ed. by Žukowsky (Teheran 1336, sh/1958), p. 109, 9.
2. Ṭūsī, Naṣīr ud-dīn, *Auṣāf al- ashrāf*, ed. Naṣrullāh-i Taqwā (Teheran 1306

sh/1927), pp. 14–15. Junaid, 'Rasā'il', in: *The Life, Personality and Writings of al-Junaid,* by Ali Hassan Abdel-Kader, Gibb Memorial Series, New Series XXII, (London, 1962), p. 49 ult.

3. Ghazzālī, Abū Ḥāmid Muḥammad, *Iḥyā' ^{c}ulūm ad-dīn*, 1–4 (Cairo, 1358h/1939), I, p. 311, 15.
4. According to Ḥasan ibn ^{c}Alī al-Muṭawwi^{c}ī.—Ibn al-Jauzī, Abū'l Faraj, *Dhamm al-hawā*, ed. Muṣṭafā ^{c}Abd al-Wāḥid (Cairo, 1381h/1962), p. 27, 16.
5. According to Anonymous, Tahānawī, Muḥammad ^{c}Alī ibn ^{c}Alī, *Kashshāf iṣṭilāḥāt al-funūn*, ed. Nassau Lees, Sprenger *et al.*, 1–2 (Calcutta, 1854–62), 2, p. 1156.
6. Ghazzālī, *Iḥyā'* I, p. 173, 4–5.
7. Abū ^{c}Alī ibn al-Kātib, d. after 340/951.–Sulamī, Abū ^{c}Abd ar Raḥmān, *Ṭabaqāt aṣ-Ṣūfiya*, ed. Johannes Pedersen (Leiden 1960), pp. 401, 8–9.
8. Abū Sulaimān ad-Dārāni, d. 215h/830).—Anṣārī, ^{c}Abdullāh-i Harawī, *Ṭabaqāt aṣ-Ṣūfiya*, ed. ^{c}Abd ul-Ḥayy-i Ḥabībī (Kabul 1340sh/1961), p. 39, 6–7.
9. Abū 'l-Ḥasan al-Muzayyin, d. 328 h/939–40.—*Sulamī, Ṭabaqāt*, p. 399, 11–12.
10. Acc. to Abū'l-Ḥusain an-Nūrī, d. 294 h/907–8.—Ansārī, *Ṭabaqāt* p. 62 below.
11. Acc. to Bāyezīd (= Abū Yazīd al-Bisṭāmī), d. 261 h/875.—Sahlajī, *An-nūr min kalimāt Abī Ṭaifūr*, in: Badawī, ^{c}Abd ar-Rahmān, Shaṭaḥāt aṣ-Sūfiya (Cairo 1949). p. 85, 9–10; 86, 4–5, Sulamī, Ṭabaqāt, p. 64, 10–12.
12. Maibudī, Abū'l-Faḍl Rashīd ud-dīn, *Kashf ul-asrār wa-^{c}uddat ul-abrār*, ed. ^{c}Alī Aṣghar-i Ḥikmat, 1–10, Teheran 1130 sh/1954–1339 sh/1960), V, p. 208.
13. Sahlajī, *An-nūr* p. 85, 1–6.
14. Ghazzālī, Iḥyā' IV p. 240, 18.
15. Thus Abū Bakr, ^{c}Āmir ibn ^{c}Abd Qais, Muḥammad ibn Wāsi^{c}, Ḥallāj.—Firkāwī, Maḥmūd, *Sharḥ Manāzil as-sā'irīn*, ed. De Beaureceuil (Cairo, 1953), pp, 151 pu.; Jullābī, *Kashf ul-maḥjūb* pp. 111–12; 428, 1–2; Akhbār al-Ḥallāj, ed. L. Massignon 3rd. ed. (Paris, 1957), p. 16; Rūzbihān-i Baqlī, *Sharḥ-i shaṭḥiyāt*, ed. H. Corbin, *Bibliothèque iranienne* 12 (Teheran-Paris 1344 sh/1966) pp. 74, 14.
16. Ghazzālī, *Iḥyā'* I p. 295, 20–21.
17. Kubrā, Najm ud-din, *Fawā'iḥ al-ǧamāl wa fawātiḥ al-ǧalāl*, ed. Fritz Meier (Wiesbaden, 1957), No. 99.
18. Acc. to ^{c}Āmir ibn ^{c}Abd Qais, d. under *Mu^{c}āwiya* (41h./661–60h./680).—Tirmidhī, Abū ^{c}Abdallāh al-Ḥakīm, *aṣ-ṣalāh wamaqāṣiduhā*, ed. ^{c}Abd al-Ḥalīm Maḥmūd and Ḥusnā Naṣr Zaidān (Cairo, 1965), p. 57, 11–12.

19. Acc. to Abū Manṣūr al-Isfāhānī, *Nahj al-khāṣṣ*, Mélanges Taha Hussein (Cairo, 1962), p. 56, 4–5.
20. Sha^{c}rānī, ^{c}Abd al-Wahhāb, *Al-anwār al-qudsiyya fī ma^{c}rifat qawā'id aṣ-Ṣūfiya,* ed. Ṭaha ^{c}Abd al-Bāqī Surūr and Muḥammad ^{c}Īd ash-Shāfi^{c}ī (Cairo, 1962) I, p. 114, 1–3.
21. Sulamī, Ṭabaqāt p. 346, 7–8; ^{c}Aṭṭār, Farīd ud-dīn, *Tadhkirat ul- auliyā'*, ed. R. A. Nicholson, 1–2 (London & Leiden, 1905–17), II, 179, p. 14–15.
22. Sarrāj' Abū Naṣr, *Kitāb al-luma^c fī't-taṣawwuf*, ed. R. A. Nicholson (London & Leiden 1914), p. 398, 7–8; Rūzbihān, *Sharḥ-i Shaṭḥiyāt*, p. 234, 10–11.
23. Sarrāj, *Luma^c*, p. 192, 4–5.
24. Sha^{c}rānī, ^{c}Abd al-Wahhāb, *Aṭ-ṭabaqāt al-kubrā*, 1–2 (Cairo, 1343, h/1925, I, p. 90, 12–123; ^{c}Aṭṭār, *Tadhkira* II, pp. 169, 9–11; Faṣīḥ-i Khwāfī, Aḥmad ibn Jalāl ud-dīn-i Muḥammad, *Mujmal-i Faṣīḥī*, ed. Mahmūd-i Farrukh, 1–3 (Mashhad, 1339—40 sh/1961), II p. 58.
25. Dīwān Abī Bakr ash-Shiblī, ed. Kāmil Muṣṭafā ash-Shaybī (Baghdad 1386, h/1967), No. 47.
26. Dhū'n-Nūn al-Miṣrī, d. 245 h/860.—Sarrāj, *Luma^c* p. 28, 11–12; Qushairī, *Risāla* (Cairo 1367 h/1948), p. 125, 18–19 bāb at-tauḥīd.
27. Abū Sulaimān ad-Dārānī, d. 215 h/830.—Abū Ṭālib al-Makkī. *Qūt al-qulūb*, I–4 (Cairo 1351 h/1932) III, p. 129, 8–10, dhikr faḍā'il shahādat at-tauḥīd.
28. Abū Bakr al-Wāsiṭī, d. 320 h/932.—Sulamī, Abū ^{c}Abd ar-Raḥmān, *Tafsīr,* ad Sura 14, Ms. Fatih 262, fol. 104 b-104 a.
29. Sura 16:37.
30. Sulamī, *Tafsīr*, ad. Sura 16, Ms. *Fatih*, fol, 112b, 6–3 from bottom.
31. Sikandarī, Ibn ^{c}Aṭā'allāh, *at-tanwīr fī isqāṭ at-tadbīr,* (Cairo 1345, h/1926–27), pp. 8, 25–26.
32. Abū ^{c}Abdallāh ibn al- Jallā', d. 306 h/918.—Sulamī, *Ṭabaqāt* pp. 168, 5–6.
33. Abū Bakr ash-Shiblī, d. 334/1946—Anṣarī, *Ṭabaqāt* pp. 543, 9–10.
34. Sahl at- Tustarī, d. 283 h/896 or 273 h/886–7, and others.—See B. Reinert, *Die Lehre vom tawakkul in der klassischen Sufik* (Berlin, 1968), pp. 96 ff.
35. Junaid, Abū'l-Qāsim ibn Muḥammad, d. 297h. or 298 h/910 or 911 -Sarrāj, *Luma^c* p. 29, *loc. cit.*
36. Sahl at-Tustarī.—Sahl ibn ^{c}Abdallāh at-Tustarī, *Tafsīr al-qur'ān al-^{c}aẓīm* (Cairo, 1329 h/1911) pp. 49–50; Qushairi, *Risāla*, p. 76, 77, 3, *bāb at-tawakkul.*
37. Sahl at-Tustarī.—Qushairī, Risāla 76, 11–13, *bāb at-tawakkul*; Suhrawardī, Abū Ḥafṣ ^{c}Umar, *^{c}Awārif al-ma^{c}ārif* (Cairo, 1358h/1939), pp. 347, 4–6, *et seq.*
38. Acc. to Junaid.—Sarrāj, *Luma^c* p. 29, 7; Junaid, *Rasā'il*, p. 14–15.

39. Jalāl ud-dīn Rūmī, *Mathnawī-i ma^{c}nawī, The Mathnawi of Jalālu'ddīn Rūmī,* R. A. Nicholson, Gibb Memorial Series, NS IV, 1–8 (London 1925–1940), I 1787.
40. Acc. to Shiblī and/or Junaid.—Kalābādhī, Abū Bakr Muḥammad ibn Ishāq *At-ta^{c}arruf li-madhhab at-taṣawwuf*, ed. A. J. Arberry (Cairo, 1934), p. 72, 4; Sarrāj, *Luma^{c}* p. 52, 18; Suhrawardi, *^{c}Awārif*, pp. 346, 20–31; ^{c}Aṭṭār, *Tadhkira* II, pp. 31, 7–8.
41. Ghazzālī, *Iḥyā'* IV p. 242, 3–8. *Kitāb at-tauḥīd wa't-tawakkul, bayān ḥaqīqat at-tauḥīd*, etc.—Concretely: 'If it came into my mind that Hell with its fire and its flame could burn a single one of my hairs, I would be a polytheist'. (Shiblī, in: Sarraj, *Luma^{c}* p. 406, 7–8).
42. Junaid.—Sarrāj, *Luma^{c}* p. 29, 2–3.
42. Sulamī, Ṭabaqāt p. 144–5; Abū Nu^{c}aim al-Iṣfahānī, *Hilyat al-auliyā*, 1–10 (Cairo 1351h–57h/1932–38), X p. 278; Suhrawardī, *^{c}Awārif* p. 58, chap. 9.
44. Ibn ^{c}Arabī, *Al-futūḥāt al-Makkiyya*, 1–4 (Cairo 1329h/1911), II, p. 513, 18.
45. Cf. Kharrāz, *Abū Sa^{c}īd Aḥmad ibn ^{c}Īsā*, d. 277h/890–1.—Anṣāī *Ṭabaqāt* p. 561, 1.
46. Ruwaim ibn Aḥmad, d. 303h/915–16.—Sarrāj, *Luma^{c}* pp. 31, 18; Anṣārī, Ṭabaqāt pp. 172, 3–4.
47. Junaid.—Qushairī, *Risāla* pp. 136, 14.
48. Wāsiṭī.—^{c}Aṭṭār, *Tadhkira* II pp. 269, 15–17.
49. Bāyezīd.—Sahlagī, *An-nūr* p. 125.
50. Junaid.—^{c}Attār, *Tadhkira* II pp. 7, 9.
51. Ja^{c}far aṣ-Ṣādiq, d. 148/765.—Sulamī, *Tafsīr ad Sura* 20:12, fol. 139 a.
52. Cf. Junaid, *Kitāb al-fanā'*, in: *Rasā'il* p. 33, 14 ff.
53. id. p. 32, 12–14.
54. id. p. 34, 3 from bottom.
55. Abū ^{c}Alī ad-Daqqāq.— ^{c}Aṭṭār, *Tadhkira* II p. 197–8.
56. Rūmī, *Mathnawī* V 2022.
57. Bāyezīd.—Sahlagī, *An-Nūr* p. 77, 118, 1; Bīrūnī, Abū'r-Raiḥān Muhammad ibn Aḥmad, *Taḥqīq mā lil-Hind min maqūla maqbūla fī'l-^{c}aql au mardhūla* (Hyderabad/Deccan 1958), pp. 67, 1–2.
58. Ḥallāj, Ḥusain ibn Manṣūr, d. 309/922.—Massignon, Louis, Le *Dīwān d'al-Hallaj* (Paris 1955). p. 103 bottom.
59. Abū Sa^{c}īd -i Abū'l-Khair, d. 440/1049.—Muḥammad ibn Munawwar, *Asrār ut-tauḥīd fi maqāmāt ish-shaikh Abī Sa^{c}īd*, ed. Dhabīḥullāh-i Ṣafā (Teheran, 1332sh/1954), p. 259 bottom.
60. For the recasting by steps of the confessional formula, see *Risāla-i-ṣafīr-i Sī murgh*, in: Spies-Khatak, *Three Treatises on Mysticism*, by Shihābuddīn Suhrawardī Maqtūl (Stuttgart, 1935), p. 27–9.
61. Zain ul-^{c}ābidīn-i Shīrwānī, *Bustān us-siyāḥa* (Teheran 1315-sh/1936). p. 328, 9–10.

62. Mark the pun *wujūd-numūd* (Reality-appearance, 'Sein und Schein') in Ṣafī[c]alīshāh, Ḥājj Mīrzā Ḥasan, *[c]Irfān ul-ḥaqq* (Teheran 1333 sh/1954), p. 5.
63. In the language of the mystics, 'reality' (*ḥaqīqa*) does not mean the world of profane experience, but rather the world of God, the mystical world which lies beyond everyday experience, and which is set over against the profane, which is a metaphor (*majāz*).
64. Anonymous.—Sarrāj, *Luma*[c] p. 32, 7–8; cf. Qushairī, *Risāla,* p. 136, 28, *bāb at-tauḥīd.*
65. Anṣārī, *Ṭabaqāt*, pp. 173, 1–2.
66. Shiblī.—Qushairī, Risāla p. 125, 33, *bāb at-tauḥīd.* Cf. Ibn Qayyim al-Jauziyya, *Madārij as-sālikīn*, ed. Muḥammad Hāmid al-Fīqī, 1–3 (Cairo 1375h/1955–6) III p. 514, 6: 'The profession of unity is his quality and his word which is constantly extant in him'.
67. Ḥallāj.—*Akhbār al-Ḥallāj*, ed. L. Massignon and Paul Kraus, 3rd. ed., Paris 1957, p. 93 No. 62.
68. Anṣārī, Abdallāh, *Manāzil as-sā'irīn*, ed. de Beaureceuil, (Cairo, 1962) p. 113.
69. Various variants are ascribed to various personalities, Dhū' n-Nūn al-Miṣrī; Kalābādhī, *Ta[c]arruf* p. 105, 2; 2) Junaid; Sarrāj, *Luma*[c] p. 29, 11, 30, 1–2; Qushairī, *Risāla* p. 135–6, *bāb at-tauḥīd*; similarly *Rasā'il* p. 2, 11; 3) Shiblī; *[c]Aṭṭār, Tadhkira* II p. 175, 17–18.
70. Sarrāj, *Luma*[c] p. 30, 3 a.o.; cf. Note 40.
71. Shiblī.—Al-Khaṭīb al-Baghdādī, Abū Bakr Aḥmad ibn [c]Alī, *Ta'rīkh Baghdād*, 1–14 (Cairo 1349 h/1931), XIV, p. 390, 12–13.
72. Shiblī.—Qushairī, [c]Abd al-Karīm, *at-taḥbīr fī't-tadhkīr*, ed. Ibrāhīm Basyūnī (Cairo 1968), p. 23, 5–6.

Creation and Judgment in the Koran and in Mystico-Poetical Interpretation

Annemarie Schimmel

Some time ago I had to examine a candidate in Oxford who had submitted a four-volume thesis on the Development of Tomb Towers in Iran up to the sixteenth century. One of the questions that arose during the defence of the thesis was the quite permissible one of the extent to which the building of tombs for rulers and saints could be reconciled with Islamic ideas of death and judgment. The veneration of the dead and even excessive weeping for the deceased, let alone the erection of pompous monuments as memorials for rulers or religious leaders, were alien to early Islam, and many Prophetic traditions are quoted against such an un-Islamic custom. Reformers in more recent times have directed their attacks against exaggerated manifestations of mourning, and even more against the veneration of tombs which had become one of the central features in later popular Sufism. Among the customs they particularly abhorred were the frequent visits of women to cemeteries, which gave them the rare opportunity of an outing.

It is possible that the central rôle of death and judgment in the earliest Islamic revelations had caused an aversion to the outspoken and exaggerated interest in and veneration of burial places in early Islam. Allah had revealed Himself to the Prophet at the beginning of the Koran as the Creator, who created man from one drop of blood (Sura 91 : 1 f.) and at the same time as the Judge who one day would call the same human being into His presence to ask him whether he had fulfilled the obligations of his religion. Creator, Sustainer and Judge are the three aspects of the one God; for He can be only one in whose hands creation and judgment lie, and who sustains and nourishes men most miraculously during their brief stay on earth. 'Which of the blessings of your Lord will you both deny?' is the refrain of Sura 55, which bears the title *Sūrat ar-Raḥmān*, The Merciful. The hour of judgment can come tomorrow, as the Koran repeats many a time (Sura 54:26 and others); therefore Persian mystical poets have often spoken of the one day of life which lies between *dūsh*, 'yesterday' (that is, the beginning of creation) and *fardā*, 'tomorrow' (that is, the Day of Judgment).

The Koran constantly stresses the marvel of creation. Creation is a unique event by which God has called the world into being. His creative word *kun*, 'Be!', brings it forth from non-existence into existence (Sura 2:111). It makes basically no difference whether this bringing into existence is seen as happening in a fixed number of days (Sura 7:52: six days) or over a span of time: in either case creation originates from the unique Divine word which, as was recently said, goes out from God in a linear movement and leads to a particular goal. Creation and Judgment are the two poles of the world which human beings can experience. Before creation lies *azal*, eternity without beginning; after Judgment, *abad*, eternity without end, which a Muslim might well understand in the imagery of the Christian hymn:

O eternity, word of thunder,
O sword that pierces the soul,
O beginning without end . . .

Yet, the possibility is open, and has been developed theologically, that God creates everything anew in every moment, so that the continuous appearance of things consists in reality of a constant creation, which is very subtly fragmented and permanently renewed. It is God's custom, his *sunna*, to make this creation appear continuous, permanent and almost unchangeable, although it is renewed in every moment. That is why a miracle is called *khāriq ul-ᶜāda*, 'what pierces the custom': that is, what changes the sequence of events without outward cause. This theory, mainly elaborated by the Ashᶜarite school, shows God as the absolute creator without secondary causes: fire can burn only if He permits it, otherwise it will not hurt man. A painting by the Pakistani artist Sadiqain expresses the mystery of creation in a calligraphic image: he has written the words *kun fa-yakūn*, 'Be! and it becomes', in the shape of a spiral nebula, the basic form in creation. From the rotating ends of the two final letters *n*, sun, stars and moons pour forth to become the world. In this calligraphic painting, God's creativity, which is unique and yet continuous, is so beautifully symbolized that Sadiqain's picture becomes an illustration of the words of the Indo-Muslim philosopher-poet Muhammad Iqbal who speaks of the inexhaustible possibilities of Divine activities: 'The Not-Yet of God means unfailing realization of the infinite creative possibilities of His being which retains its wholeness throughout the entire process'.

Of course Islamic philosophers and mystics have invented a number of different theories about creation. They have postulated an emanation from an eternal reality which is substantially no more different from God than ice is from water, and they have seen creation as the pouring out of existence upon possibilities which were only potentially existent and now became real to a certain extent, just as colourless glass, when struck by invisible light, becomes visible and thus 'real'. The latter theory was acceptable to some orthodox mystics, such as the later Naqshbandiyya; but the doctrine of Unity of Being, as first elaborated theoretically by Ibn ᶜArabī (d. 1240) was always rejected by orthodox theologians, at least in its popularized expression *hama ōst*, 'Everything is He'—an oversimplification which omitted the complex detail of Ibn ᶜArabī's theories. Other mystics found in the words of the profession of faith a subtle hint of a continuous creation: the emanation of created things which are to some extent different from God is expressed by the *Lā ilāh*, 'There is no deity', while their return to Him is alluded to by the second half of the sentence, *illā Allāh*, 'save God'. Creation is seen here as the Divine breath that keeps everything alive and takes it back to its origin. In his *Ushturnāma*, Farīduddīn ᶜAṭṭār, the great mystical poet of Nishapur (d. 1220), was among the first Sufis to use the symbol of the shadow-play for human life. The same symbol was used a little later by the Arabic mystical poet Ibn al-Fāriḍ (d. 1235) in his long mystical ode, the *Tā'iyat al-kubrā*. God takes the puppets out of the box of non-existence, moves them about, makes them play, and finally casts them again into the darkness of unqualified unity. But even in a puppet play the good are recompensed and the bad punished, as a later Naqshbandi mystic in India, Khwāja Mīr Dard (d. 1785), has expressly stated. ᶜAṭṭār's compatriot Shihābuddīn Suhrawardī 'Maqtūl' (executed 1191) invented a grand system of creation which is not always compatible with orthodox ideas. According to him, the world comes into existence by the sound of Gabriel's wing; and his angelology, as much as his philosophy of illumination, is one of the most fascinating things in Islamic mystical philosophy.

The idea of a necessary constant perfection of the created world logically results from the historical view determined by the two limits of creation and judgment. The religion brought by Muhammad as the last, and that means the most perfect, message in the long line of prophetic revelations is at the same time the eternal, primordial religion which existed in the Divine will and knowledge, and which had been made known time and again fragmentarily. This idea of completion and perfection of the world was expressed by the mystical poets in particularly impressive imagery. In the Middle Ages, ᶜAṭṭār describes in his *Manṭiq uṭ-Ṭair* how infinite numbers of creatures are annihilated until the one being can be born for whom creation has been hoping and longing from its very beginning. In our own time Iqbal has used these poetical images to show that hundreds of gardens have to perish until the one longed-for rose, the Prophet, appears in the garden of this world. The growth of created beings through various levels of manifestation was often expressed by Maulānā Jalāluddīn Rūmī (d. 1273) in his *Mathnawī*; the most famous passage of this kind is in Vol. III, verse 3901. It was translated by Rückert into German as early as in the 1830s (without, however, quoting the last, decisive line); the best English version is R. A. Nicholson's:

I died as mineral and became a plant,
I died as plant and rose to animal.
I died as animal and I was Man.
Why should I fear? When was I less by dying?
Yet once more I shall die as Man, to soar
With angels blest: but even from angelhood
I must pass on: all except God doth perish.
When I have sacrificed my angel-soul
I shall become what no mind e'er conceived.
O let me not exist! For Non-existence
Proclaims in organ tones 'To Him we shall return!'

The ascent of man ends in *ᶜadam*, which can best be translated as 'positive not-being' which means, in Rūmī's terminology, the eternal and unfathomable abyss of the Divine Essence. We should not understand these lines, as is often done, as pointing to a mechanical development to higher levels of being but read them in their context, for all relevant passages in Rumi's work contain allusions to the truth that development and progress can be attained only by self-sacrifice. Even the chick-pea that offers itself to man as food and suffers in boiling water in order finally to partake in man of a higher level of existence is connected with one of Rumi's favourite quotations: the beginning of a poem by the Baghdadian martyr mystic Ḥallāj:

Kill me, O my trustworthy friends,
for in my being killed there is my life . . .

These are words which prefigure Goethe's *Stirb und werde*, 'Die and come to be!' an aphorism whose motif, the story of moth and candle, indeed goes back to this very mystic's *Kitāb aṭ-ṭawāsīn*, as H. H. Schaeder has proved.

Apart from the unshakable faith in a *creatio ex nihilo* by God's creative word, the central concept of Islamic theories of creation is the statement in Sura 7:171 which has been interpreted from early times as the proof of the pre-eternal covenant between God and man. There are doubts as to whether or not the Koran really intends such a deep meaning; but mystically-inclined Muslims have interpreted the line in this way, and made it a cornerstone of their theological approach. Henri Corbin rightly says that the Islamic concept of history is founded upon a meta-historical event. He refers to the scene where God took the future mankind out of the loins of the as yet uncreated Adam, addressing them thus, *alastu bi-rabbikum*, 'Am I not your Lord?' and they answered *balā, shahidnā*, 'Yes, we bear testimony'. These were the first words uttered to anything created, and in doing so God revealed Himself as the Lord of the world. On the last day He will ask mankind whether they have been faithful to their promise by giving witness to God's sovereignty in the world whenever his messengers have reminded them of this primordial covenant. It is typical of the radical attitude of the early Sufis, with their absolute submission to God's inscrutable will, that Ghazzālī, the great medieval theologian, combines this Koranic sentence with the famous fatalist tradition according to which God said 'Those to Hell, and I do not care, and these for Paradise, and I do not care'.

The mystics describe the *bazm-i alast*, the 'banquet of pre-eternity', as it is called in the Persian cultural tradition, in terms of ever-new images. For them it means the day on which souls drank the wine of Divine love for the first time, the day when they were elected to be not only absolutely obedient but to participate in the mystery of essential Divine love. With the word *balā*, 'Yes', they accepted every tribulation that God would send on them as a sign of His love, for *balā* also means 'affliction'. The *dhikr* of the dervishes, the central devotional act of recollecting God, reminds the pious of this first Divine address and therefore leads the soul to the moment when there was nothing but God alone. Maulānā Rūmī has described the miracle of *alast* with an unusual though beautiful image: Not-being heard God's address and became so intoxicated that it entered the world of being in a jubilant dance, manifesting itself in tulips, willows, and herbs. For Rūmī, the mystical dance, *samā*^{c}, is the repetition of the act of creation in which birth and death in love are one and the same.

Creation is also the separation of creatures from God. It is then that a directed time comes into existence; a time which, like the constantly active Divine word, extends between pre-eternity and endless eternity, and thus forms a limit which man can surpass only in rare moments of ecstasy. For the mystics the word which the Prophet spoke during his ascension to heaven, e.g. 'I have a time (*kairos*, moment) with God in which even Gabriel has no access', is proof of the fact that it is possible to break through created serial time and to share in the Divine *nunc aeternum*. Such a breakthrough is, however, granted only to the most perfected human beings, but not to the—static—angels.

But what is the meaning of creation? The Koran answers: Everything is created to worship God and to serve Him in veneration. Adoration, service of God in the true sense of the word, is the meaning of creation and thus of history. This is indicated by the word of the primordial covenant of *alast*; it has to be realized and manifested in the life of every single individual, and even in the life of nations. But the command is also intended for the lower ranks of creatures: for stones, plants, and animals which, like the angels, are constantly occupied with worship, expressing their praise and adoration in silent eloquence by their whole being and action. Few passages in mystical literature of the Muslim peoples are more impressive than the prayers in which the mystics have translated this constant worship of everything created into human language. Dhū'n-Nūn, a ninth-century Egyptian mystic, seems to have been the first who, after the period of early anti-world asceticism, expressed the hymns of everything created which permeate the world. Dhū'n-Nūn's prayers and hymns have been echoed hundreds of times in later Islamic poetry, whether in the long chains of anaphora with which ᶜAṭṭār fills his epic poems, or in moving folk legends, or in rich and colourful odes which usually begin with the praise of God whose wisdom and power manifest themselves through the interplay of contradictory manifestations in nature and fate until the poet eventually turns to the Lord, addressing him as Thou, and opening his heart before him in full trust and in hope of his mercy.

The meaning of creation can be seen from another viewpoint:

that of a *ḥadīth qudsī* that was a favourite with mystics throughout the centuries: *kuntu kanzan makhfiyyan* ... 'I was a hidden treasure and wanted to be known, therefore I created the world'. God, unhappy to be alone in His absolute beauty and majesty, wanted someone to enjoy and admire His attributes; therefore He created the world as a mirror, or as the place for the manifestation of His eternal Beauty. Not only veneration and adoration are due to Him, but love, for beauty causes love. The *ḥadīth* of the hidden treasure is one of the essentials of later Islamic mystical poetry; it then becomes a problem of interpretation whether to maintain God's absolute transcendence knowing that, whereas man needs God for his existence, God does not need anything, for 'He is the needless Rich, but you are the needy' (Sura 36:40). On the other hand, one might speak with the school of Ibn ᶜArabī of a longing and desiring God who in a certain way needs man and creation so that His names and attributes can be properly reflected. The borderlines between the various approaches are necessarily vague, and can barely be defined in due theological terms.

The idea that God follows man with His mercy and love in every moment of life was expressed by the Iraqi mystic Niffari in the tenth century in a text which its editor, A. J. Arberry, has rightly compared with Francis Thompson's *Hound of Heaven*. From here it is not far to Rūmī's famous:

> Not only the thirsty long for water,
> Water also longs for the thirsty (*Mathnawī* I 1704)

—a verse repeated even in eighteenth-century Sindhi poetry. We often find similar sentences in the words of Ibn ᶜArabī's followers, words which sound as if they were taken from Angelus Silesius' poetry or from the first chapter of Rilke's *Book of Hours*. But even a contemporary Muslim philosopher such as Muhammad Iqbal, who was a merciless critic of medieval pantheistic mysticism in Islam says in his *Zabūr-i ᶜAjam* (Persian Psalms):

> We have gone astray from God;
> He is searching upon the road

For like us, He is need entire
And the prisoner of desire (trans. A. J. Arberry)

This is a far cry from the scholastic definitions of God's forty-one qualities in the traditional catechisms which limit the dynamic creator-God by enclosing Him in exact formulations.

The notion of 'hidden treasure' is central to Sufism but since it is not found in the Koran it need not be accepted by the faithful as binding truth. The Koranic statement about the *amāna*, the 'entrusted good' (Sura 33:72) is more widely relevant: when God created the world he offered something in trust to heaven and earth. They refused to accept it, but man took it, yet proved ignorant and tyrannical; he did not properly know what to do with this treasure. The orthodox might understand the *amāna* as man's duty to believe and to surrender to God's will, a duty which man constantly forgets; the mystics might see here the secret of love which works through creation but can attain perfection only in man, for mountains would melt under its burden:

You created man for the pain of love—
You have your angels for obedience (Khwāja Mīr Dard)

Others, particularly the modernists, speak of the trust of free will; whereas angels and infra-human creatures live according to the form and direction that has been given to them once for all, man has been granted the rather dubious gift of free will. Or the trust may be the position of Divine vicegerency, which was granted to Adam (Sura 2:28), and which he did not always use to the best. This trust would have enabled him to perfect God's creation and to rule it; but he forgot this prerogative again and again and neglected his God-given duties. Iqbal sees in the *amāna* the possibility of individualization: the unfolding of all the possibilities that are contained in the individual until he reaches perfection, or a stage as close as possible to it. This idea is close to some theories advanced by the German philosopher Rudolf Pannwitz.

The creation story has been embellished by later generations with ever-new details. It is neither necessary nor possible in this chapter to dwell upon all the mythological ideas which have grown out of the Koranic statement that man was created from clay and formed by God's hands (Sura 38:72). The mystics invented their own myths to show how heart, spirit, and soul were created before the body and how they relate to each other. There are many fascinating creation myths in popular Islam. One of the most important points in later elaborations of the creation myth is the idea that the Prophet Muḥammad was created even before Adam, for his innermost being derives from the eternal light. The *nūr muḥammadī*, the Muhammadan Light, is the first manifestation of the Divine light, as Ḥallāj said in his *Kitāb aṭ-ṭawāsīn* shortly after 900:

> All the lights of the prophets emerge from his light; he was before all; his name was the first in the book of history; he was known before everything and to all creatures, and will last after they have faded away . . ..

The light of the Prophet appears in subsequent generations of prophets and continues, according to Shia doctrine, through the imāms, but has found its most perfect manifestation in the historical Muḥammad. When the mystical poet of Ghazna, Sanā'ī (d. ca. 1131), says:

> Although according to the form Adam was earlier than Muḥammad,
> Yet according to the meaning he was dependent upon Muḥammad,

this is merely a poetical version of the oft-quoted *ḥadīth* 'I was a prophet while Adam was still between water and clay'. The Divine tradition in which God addresses the Prophet by the word *laulāka*, 'If you had not been I would not have created the heavens', serves to explain the belief that Muḥammad's essence was created before everything else, for he is the meaning and end of creation. Such ideas led sometimes in later periods to mystical theories amazingly similar to logos speculations in Christian theology. However, this development is quite alien to Muḥammad's own conception of his rôle, for he, in accordance with Koran Sura 18:110, had always underlined that he was nothing but a servant to whom it was revealed.

As for Adam, the first man and first prophet, the story of his creation is told several times in the Koran. God taught him the names (Sura 2:31). As the first recipient of the Divine message, he was destined to become the lord of names and named things. That is why the angels prostrated themselves before him, for this mystery of the names was not unveiled to them. One of them, however, refused to bow down before a created being: it was Iblīs, who referred to his fiery origin and to his long-standing service. The figure of Iblīs, Satan—who is seen in Islam always as the enemy of man, but never as God's adversary—has fascinated many Muslim mystics. Ḥallāj was the first to present Satan's refusal to bow down before Adam as an expression of love of God and his true obedience: '*juḥūdī laka taqdīs*: my rebellion means to declare Thee holy', thus Ḥallāj translates Satan's viewpoint. God had ordered by His eternal order that no one should prostrate himself before anything save God. But how was this order compatible with the expression of His will, created in this moment, that Adam should be an object of prostration? Seen from this aspect, Satan becomes for certain mystics 'more monotheist than God Himself', as Hellmut Ritter puts it. He becomes the martyr to obedience. Aḥmad Ghazzālī (d. 1126) sees him as the great lover, and one of the most touching poems of the Ghaznawid mystic, Sanā'ī, expresses the complaint of the exiled angel, who could boast of so many ages of obedience and yet was exiled by a Divine ruse, for Adam acted as the grain in the Divine snare (just as Satan was to seduce Adam by a grain). Even in eighteenth-century Sindhi poetry, one finds the exclamation *ᶜāshiq ᶜazāzīl*, 'The true lover is Satan', for he preferred to be the target for the fatal arrow from the hand of his divine beloved, and surrendered to his inexplicable will. Most mystics, among them Rūmī, have of course seen Satan as the one-eyed representative of intellect and false analogy, who did not recognize the divine spark in Adam and the divine breath that had been infused into the figure of clay (Sura 5:15; 38:72); and who therefore deserves a punishment which, according to Sura 26:94, will eventually cast him into hell-fire.

In our time, Iqbal has taken up the theme of creation and the relation between man and Satan. In his series of poems called *taskhīr-i fiṭrat* in the *Payām-i Mashriq* (his answer to Goethe's *West-Östlicher Divan*), the Indo-Muslim philosopher-poet describes how the struggle between the fallen angel and man will end when man overcomes Satan who sits in his blood and manifests himself in his lower instincts. By constant 'greater holy war' against his baser qualities, man will subdue Satan and become his master, so that at the end of time Iblīs will fall down before him, prostrating himself as he was supposed to on the first day of creation. Iqbal makes Satan, 'who colours the picture of creation' by inciting man into permanent struggle, complain about the weakness and meekness of man who is all too happy to rise to his insinuations. It is the Perfect Man, the perfect servant of God, with all his thought and actions directed to the Creator, who can overcome Satan. The Prophet himself expressed this victory over the lower instincts and their transformation into positive values when he said: *Aslama shaiṭānī*: 'My Satan has surrendered to me (or, has become a Muslim) and does only what I order him to do'.

Predestination

One aspect of the Islamic theories of creation which has created considerable confusion among Muslims and their western critics is the concept of the *lauḥ maḥfūẓ* (Sura 85:22), the Well-preserved Tablet, on which the Koran and everything that is to happen are written from pre-eternity. These ideas encourage an attitude which western scholars call Islamic fatalism. Prophetic traditions such as *qad jaffa'l-qalam,* 'The Pen has dried up' (that is, nothing that has been written by the pen of Divine decree can ever be changed), have induced scholars to believe in absolute coercion, although the Koran, on the other hand, often alludes to man's free will and his capacity for action, with positive or negative results. To a great extent, the tension between the two possible interpretations of the Koranic words, i.e. in the predestinatarian sense and in favour of free will, respectively, has shaped the theological and even the political development of early Islam. The concept of the Mu^{c}tazila, a school of thought that postulated God's absolute justice at the expense of his absolute power, and eventually confronted the free human being with a Creator limited by his own justice, was probably even more difficult to defend in the long run than the deeply religious conviction that God is almighty and rules supreme in the worlds. The complexity of the Divine Names—called the Ninety-nine Most Beautiful Names of God—as they occur in the Koran, seems to reflect God's manifold activities and the unfathomable depth of his wisdom better than most theological theories.

Solutions to the problems of the well-preserved tablet and 'written' fate were sought and found in various ways. Some philosophers and mystics identified the well-preserved tablet with the active intellect, *'aql fa^{cc}āl*, or with the all-soul, *nafs-i kull.* Others, such as the followers of Ibn ^{c}Arabī's doctrine of the unity of being, saw everything, even evil, as part of God. A particularly happy answer to the problem of predestination is offered in Jalāluddīn Rūmī's interpretation of the tradition of the dried-up pen. The pen no longer writes anything new, but that does not mean that evil deeds have been predestined or can lead to a good end, but that God has ordered a particular fruit for every action. That was mentioned in the Koran and enforced in the oft-quoted prophetic tradition: 'This world is the seedbed of the Otherworld'.

> When you plant colocinth you cannot expect to harvest sugarcane. (Rūmī, *Dīwān*, Nr. 1337)

or:

> One beats the ox when he refuses to carry his yoke, not because he has not got wings. (*Mathnawī* V 3102)

Maulana Rumi's story of the man who stole fruits and told the gardener that he was acting in accordance with God's will illustrates this viewpoint; for the gardener gave him a sound beating with 'God's stick', and on God's orders, until the thief had to admit that God neither wanted nor ordered his transgression of the law (*Mathnawī* V 3077 ff.).

One should never confuse so-called Islamic fatalism with belief in a blind fate. It is not a dogmatic theory but a living religious experience. If something is *maktūb*, 'written', then that is so because God, in his eternal wisdom, knows what man needs at every moment. *Ḥusn aẓ-ẓann*, 'to think good about God', is one of the branches of absolute trust in God, a trust which is still the source of strength for millions of faithful. The pious Muslim knows that a change of his will can take place in prayer, which enables him to accept ungrudgingly, and even lovingly, events which are contrary to his own wishes and which he can learn to accept gratefully whatever God sends. In this way he reaches the high rank of *jabr maḥmūd* or praiseworthy coercion.

The problem of predestination has always puzzled the pious, and it is small wonder that innumerable poets have written on it. The nineteenth-century Indo-Muslim poet Ghalib (d. 1869) offers a most profound introduction to the question in the famous introductory verse of his *Urdu Divan*, when he says:

> The drawing is a complainant against whom, against what daring artist's hand?
> Every writing and every painting wears a paper-shirt.

God is seen here in a traditional image as the master calligrapher who writes human beings like letters by forming their various shapes from the one original ink (as the Shia mystic Ḥaidar-i Āmulī said in the fourteenth century). One letter complains that it has been written on bad paper, another may find itself together with ugly letters or on a crooked line; and each of them complains of something, for each wears a paper shirt, which means in medieval Islamic lore the shirt of the complainant when he goes to court. A letter becomes visible, of course, only after being written on paper. However, what letter would know how the completed book would look, or what its contents would be? The image is reminiscent of Rilke's sonnet about the Gardens of Isfahan, which is completely Islamic in feeling and imagery:

> To whatever picture you are united within,

even though for a moment in the life of pain:
feel that the whole, the glorious carpet is meant!

Islam is a culture strongly shaped by writing, for it introduced into the history of religions the difference between religions with a sacred book and with no written revelation. In Islam, therefore, it is normal to imagine the world and creation as a book. In the seventeenth century the Indo-Persian poet Kalīm complained about man's ignorance of the beginning and end of time:

> We do not know anything of the beginning and the end of this world,
> For the first and the last page of this ancient book are missing . . .

Yet the mind of the faithful Muslim never ceased to move between those two mysterious pages when he tried to read the script of days and nights and to decypher the histories of the bygone, written for those who had eyes to see. As a good Muslim, the reader of the book of time was aware that the necessary outcome of God's pre-eternal address to mankind is man's duty to devote his whole life to the Lord, and that he is constantly in God's most holy presence. 'To serve Him as though he were seeing Him', as the Prophetic tradition defines the concept of *iḥsān*, a word that interiorizes the basic concepts of *islām*, 'submission', and *īmān*, 'faith'. This definition of the human position in God's presence has led to casuistic definitions of every human act, including actions which one would normally consider profane. Such a codification of behaviour prescribed by the awareness of God's constant presence is a most important aspect of Muslim life. The best introduction to this kind of thinking is an Arabic work that has greatly influenced Muslim society for the last eight hundred years because it faithfully reflects its ideals: Abū, Ḥāmid Ghazzālī's (d. 1111) *Iḥyāᶜ ulūm ad-dīn*. On a close reading, this handbook of moderately mystical Islam offers a perfect picture of man's duties, which result from his pre-eternal response to God's call and his acceptance of God as the supreme ruler. Once he follows these prescriptions, he can meet God as his faithful servant at the end of time. The thirty-nine chapters of the

Iḥyā, centring on the twentieth chapter, which deals with the Prophet, lead to the fortieth and last book, which contains a description of the attitude of the pious at the hour of death.

Islamic theology has always emphasized the soul's experiences at the moment of death and between the funeral and resurrection. Nevertheless, the doctrine of punishment in the grave or of the happiness of the pious in their tombs has no firm foundation in the Koran; it developed from the prophetic traditions and was elaborated by popular theologians and preachers. In many cases, death is seen as the real fruit of life, as *hamrang*, or of the same colour as life. In the *Kindertotenlieder,* or dirges for two of his children, the German orientalist Friedrich Rückert says:

> Death is the essence of life, as the fruit is the essence of the flower:
> it was hidden in it from the very beginning and has now become unveiled from the blossom.

Rückert echoes the feelings of the Islamic mystics. Rilke's repeated references to 'dying one's own death' are also close to these ideas. In his eschatological treatise *ad-durra al-fākhira*, 'The precious pearl in the knowledge of the Otherworld', Ghazzālī has described how in the grave man's actions torment him like animals. It is a short step to the verses of his younger contemporary, Sanā'ī, the mystical poet of Ghazna, which tell how the interior attitude of man can manifest itself at Doomsday as animals; this idea is also found in ᶜAṭṭār's mystical poetry. In the Christian tradition Swedenborg's writings reveal a similar concept when he says that the last Judgment is basically an unveiling of the form which the spirit has assumed in this life, and in which will develop further in eternity. Rumi somewhat tones down the ideas of his predecessors; for him, death is a mirror which shows everyone his true face, or else the actions of man and his thoughts follow him to the Otherworld as though they were his wives and children. All men's thoughts will take shape in the Otherworld, just as the thought of an architect is eventually manifested in the outward shape of a beautiful house (*Mathnawī* I 1791).

Resurrection; Last Judgment; Paradise and Hell

Islamic theology and popular piety have elaborated the description of the future life in minute detail, for the Last Judgment occupies a central position in the early Koranic revelations. The Koran uses numerous images to describe the terrible day: it is 'The Hour' par excellence (thus forty times), the Day of Reckoning, the Breaking, the Covering, the Day of Separation. The world's last hour is described in striking imagery: the moon will be split (Sura 54:1), the earth will be rolled up like a carpet, and the mountains will look like combed wool. The earliest Muslims lived in fear of this hour, and the message of the Judgment was closer to their hearts than worldly power. The model of all later ascetics, Ḥasan al-Baṣrī (d. 728), who witnessed the expansion of the Islamic empire from the Straits of Gibraltar to Sind and Transoxiana (all in 711), is characterized thus by an historian: 'It was as if Hellfire was created only for him and 'Omar' (the only pious caliph of the Omayyad dynasty, 717–720). Not much later Ibn Abī Dunyā composed a whole treatise about those who uttered the Koranic saying 'O that I were dust and ashes!' (Sura 78:41) when they thought of the Last Judgment and the horrors of Doomsday. Tradition describes the Day of Resurrection in some detail, but none of these signs of the imminent Hour are of Koranic origin. There are thoughts on the coming of the Dajjāl, who is usually compared to the Anti-Christ of Christian tradition; and on the return of Christ, who will finally kill the Dajjāl, further the advent of the Mahdī, the one who is 'guided right'—a personality from the Prophet's family who will come 'to fill the world with justice as it is now filled with injustice'. This expectation, central to Shia faith, has had considerable political influence: many rebels who went to fight against an Islamic government for political or social reasons claimed to be the promised Mahdī; a fairly recent example of this tendency was the Mahdī, in the Sudan at the end of the nineteenth century. The details of the lives of, and the myths regarding these three major personalities and other secondary figures, belong more or less to popular Islam and cannot be derived from the oldest traditions. Even such ideas as that of the eschatological peace, when 'the lion and the lamb shall lie together' were not alien to later Islamic utopian hopes; this is clear from thirteenth-century mystical poetry (e.g., Jalāluddīn Rūmī) and from miniatures of the Jiahāngīr period, when under Mughal rule in India, in the first half of the seventeenth century, perfect peace seemed to have arrived—for some years at least.

Resurrection will be announced by Isrāfīl's trumpet. The very word *qiyāmat*, or 'resurrection', has become a key word in Islamic languages for every possible confusion and horror; that is as true of modern Turkish as of Sindhi. The earth will open to bring forth all the dead, and billions of people will await in burning heat the decision of the Divine Judgment:

> Torn their shrouds, and holding their heads in fear—
> How millions will shiver at the sound of the trumpet!

Thus Rūmī. This Last Judgment will be the final pronouncement on history; for although in the course of centuries and millennia numerous judgments have been passed on the infidels and the rebellious nations who refused to listen to the words of the God-sent messengers, at the end of time there will be a reckoning for each individual; his future destination will be fixed according to his actions.

The Meccans were sceptical when the Prophet talked to them about the possibility, and even the reality, of resurrection. But the Koranic proofs for the quickening of seemingly dead creatures were scarcely esoteric. Is not every spring a proof of resurrection? As the poets were to say: thunder announces new life as does Isrāfīl's trumpet; the rain of mercy falls on the dead dust and revives it; the ice melts just as coarse matter will melt at Doomsday; the lifeless grey desert and the naked trees put on green garments as though the inhabitants of paradise in their green robes had descended upon them, or as though God had bestowed upon them paradisical green silk robes as recompense for their patience during the winter.

Other thinkers, mainly mystics, might see this world and human life as a dream, following the Prophetic tradition, 'People are asleep, and when they die they awake'. The one day of life between the yesterday of the Primordial Covenant and the tomorrow of Doomsday passes like a dream, a dream, however, during which man is called to work, and whose interpretation we shall see at the Resurrection, when the morning splendour of eternity will rise for ever.

Since the publication of Sale's *Preliminary Discourse* in 1721, European scholars have shown more interest in the descriptions of heaven, hell, and resurrection in Islam than in other, more practical topics. The Koran uses various images to describe the eschatological instrumentarium, and the manuals of theology, such as the *Waṣiya* of Abū Ḥanīfa (d. 767), insist on the reality of all these instruments. There are the balances, on which the actions, or else the books of actions, will be weighed; there is the *ṣirāṭ*—in Koran 37:23 the way toward hell, but instead described in the tradition as the bridge over the back of hell; and there are the books, in which man's actions have been noted down by the two angelic scribes who accompany him during his lifetime. When the book is blackened by sins, man is dishonoured and worthy of condemnation; but if the book is put in his right hand, he may hope to be one of the saved. The various descriptions of the eschatological events are difficult to reconcile or to put into a logical order. There is one way to make the blackness of the books disappear: to shed copious tears of repentance, for ink is soluble in water, and can be washed off.

The day of Judgment will be long, almost endless. Poets such as Ḥāfiẓ have often compared the length of that day with all its horrors to the length of the day when they are separated from their beloved. Others, like Ṣā'ib (d. 1678) have declared that the most terrible punishment would be to see once more the faces of one's contemporaries. Some mystics rebelled against these ideas, for they felt that an extremely sensualistic description of man's sufferings at Doomsday was incompatible with God's greatness and majesty. (Ghazzālī's *Precious Pearl* is, in this respect, more a work expressing the ideas of preachers in the popular tradition than that of a genuine mystic.) In the early fourteenth century the Anatolian mystical bard Yūnus Emre asked:

> O my God, if Thou shouldst interrogate me once
> I shall give this answer:
> Though I may have sinned against myself,
> What have I done against Thee? . . .
>
> Thou hast created the scales to weigh sin—
> Do you want to cast me into the Fire?
> Scales are fitting for a merchant,
> A goldsmith, a druggist, or a peddler needs them.
> But Thou are All-Knowing and know my state.
> Dost Thou really need scales to examine me? . . .

This kind of rebellion and protest is expressed more impertinently in later Turkish Bektashi poetry: Is it really necessary for God to waste his time in weighing such rubbish as sin? Surely God should be the owner of a bath house if He has to keep hellfire burning? These are two of the questions put by ʿAzmī, a late sixteenth-century Turkish poet.

The orthodox, mystics, poets and philosophers pondered the mystery of the *barzakh* (Sura 23:103), that area which separates this world from the Otherworld and which can be imagined either as temporal or as spatial. They found various interpretations of the *aʿrāf* (Sura 7:44), the border-zone between Heaven and Hell which 'seems to be Hell for the houris, but Paradise for those pining in Hell', as Saʿdī (d. 1292) puts it. The *aʿrāf* was sometimes regarded as a kind of limbo, or as the dwelling-place of children who had died before reaching the age of discretion.

There is one hope for Muslims, however, amidst all the terrible events of Doomsday. Although, on that day 'when man flees from his brother' (Sura 80:35), everyone (including the prophets of the earlier peoples) will think only of himself, the Prophet Muhammad will come to intercede for his community in his quality as *fatā*, 'noble youth'. For pious Muslims the *shafāᶜa*, the Prophet's intercession, is an anchor of hope in every fear, although it is difficult to find any explict foundation for it in the Koran. In the Throne-verse (Sura 2:256) it is said: 'Who can intercede with Him but with His permission?' Islamic tradition developed this idea in early days, and derived it from Sura 17:86: 'Perhaps Thy lord will raise you to an honourable place'. Wherever hymns in honour of Muhammad have been written and sung, his rôle as intercessor of his community is the pivot upon which the trust and love of the faithful turn. This is well expressed by Rūmī:

> If in someone's hand is the hem of Mustafa's cloak,
> Even though he be in Hell, I would bring him to Paradise.

One of the most beautiful popular interpretations of this aspect of the Prophet as the loving intercessor is found in a poem of the great Sindhi mystic Shah ʿAbdul Latif (d. 1752). One of the chorus parts of the poem, *Sur Sārang*, in which the quickening rain as a sign of Divine grace is described in naturalistic images, and leads to Muḥammad, the manifestation of the same mercy attests the unshakable hope of the faithful:

My Prince will give me protection—
therefore my trust is in God
The Beloved will prostrate, will lament and cry—
therefore my trust is in God
Muḥammad, the pure and innocent, will intercede for his people—
therefore my trust is in God
When the trumpet sounds, the eyes all will be opened—
therefore my trust is in God
The pious will gather, and Muḥammad, full of glory—
therefore my trust is in God
Will proceed for every soul to the door of the Benefactor
therefore my trust is in God
And the Lord will honour him, and forgive us all our sins—
therefore my trust is in God

It is not difficult to find similar examples in high literature and folk poetry from various parts of the Muslim world.

In later times it was not only Muḥammad who could intercede for his community; this was also a privilege of the martyrs who enter Paradise immediately. Out of this nucleus the important idea developed that Ḥusain, the Prophet's grandson and arch-martyr of Islam (d. in Kerbela 680), would intercede for all those who shed tears for his death. The oldest Arabic Shia treatises already contained this idea, which was to be the cornerstone of the development of the Shia passion plays and passion poetry in Iran and in Muslim India. Even the Koran can appear as intercessor at Doomsday, as we read in many Arabic prayers written at the end of copies of the Koran and recited at the end of a recitation. In the course of time, popular piety endowed many persons, and eventually even pious deeds, with the power to rise at the Day of Judgment and defend the faithful.

Understandably, the forgiveness of sins was a matter of deep concern to Muslims. They looked for some hope in view of the sins they might have committed wittingly or unwittingly. The prayers of the 'preacher of hope', Yaḥyā ibn Mu'ādh of Rayy (d. 872), constantly express in short touching sighs the dialectical tension between man's consciousness of sinfulness and his trust in God's endless mercy:

> O God, I have not done anything for Paradise, and I have no strength to endure Hell—everything is left to Thy mercy!

Of course the Koran is full of descriptions of Hell, particularly in the oldest suras. The word *jahannam*, Hell, occurs no less than 77 times. The guardians of Hell drag away sinners who will suffer in the fire, and will eat the fruits of the *zaqqūm* tree (Suras 37:60; 44:43). Such dramatic scenes have been elaborated in increasingly frightening detail in popular piety. Hell might be described as an animal that was brought near while producing terrible sounds (Sura 67:8), or as a building in the shape of a funnel with seven storeys, about whose construction and topography the theologians argued. Much more important than the picturesque details of popular piety is the problem of eternal punishment. Many scholars, founding their ideas on Sura 23:105, were convinced that punishment would be eternal. There were more, however, who relied on Sura 11:109, to the effect that the infidels would stay in Hell for ever 'unless God decided differently'. It was thought that a favourable divine decision of that kind would probably be due to God's mercy. Besides, Hell was something created, not something co-eternal with God; therefore, it would have an end, and certainly every Muslim would be saved in the end. The Ash'arites defended this theory against the Mu'tazilites. Eventually, one tradition claimed that Hell was even afraid of the light of the true believer, for he would be surrounded by the uncreated light of God, which is able to extinguish the created fire of Hell. Others attributed this miracle to the light of Muḥammad:

> If your heart is filled with the light of Aḥmad,
> be assured that you are safe from hell fire. (Sanā'ī)

Even more colourful than the descriptions of Hell are those of Paradise—whose sensual appearance was especially helpful to Christian theologians in their anti-Muslim polemics. Paradise is a garden as wide as heaven and earth, where the faithful wear precious garments and walk at their leisure. Immaculate and immortal youths and virgins surround them, and they will drink sweet wine which causes neither drunkenness nor headache. Pavilions and fountains, rivers and copious fruits will be there, and every wish will be fulfilled. Dwelling on these Koranic remarks, popular piety has enlarged every word with hundreds of details. The word *ṭūbā*, 'being pleased' (Sura 13:39), was transformed into a marvellous tree whose elegant shape became a poetic image of the beauty of the beloved. The Prophet will abide by the *Sidra* tree at the limits of created Paradise. *Riḍwān*, God's pleasure, without which nobody can enter Paradise, was personified as the doorkeeper who allows the souls to enter (although Sura 39:73 suggests several doorkeepers). The plentitude, *kauthar*, promised to the Prophet in Sura 108, became a sweet well or fountain whose refreshing water is distributed, according to Shia interpretation, by 'Ali. Popular piety speculated on the number of houses and houris the pious Muslim would find if he faithfully carried out this or that religious supererogatory duty, or recited a formula seven, forty, or a hundred times every day. The poets usually thought it safer to drink already on earth *sharāban ṭahūran*, the 'pure wine' which was promised to the faithful in Paradise (Sura 76:40).

Muslim architects tried to imitate Paradise in this world. The *chahārbāgh*, as it is known from Persian and Indian gardens, reflects the four rivers of Paradise which 'flow in enclosed gardens' (Sura 39:7). Numerous mausoleums are erected in the middle of a *chahārbāgh* where canals cross one another so that the person who rests in the tomb can already enjoy a foretaste of that 'paradise under which rivers flow'. The construction of many gardens in eight-fold terraces, or on an eight-fold pattern, goes back to the idea of Paradise; it is assumed that Paradise has eight doors, one more than Hell, for God's mercy is greater than his wrath. The octagonal pavilions in the Mughal gardens in India may also be interpreted as reminiscences of Paradise, as the court poets described them.

The use of the number eight may have developed out of the description of the heavenly meadows in Sura 55, where two paradises are mentioned which are then duplicated. Like Hell, Paradise has been a topic for topographical research by many preachers and mystics up to our time who relied on the various names of Paradise found in the Koran. Even as great a theosophist as Ibn 'Arabī has described the three gardens of Paradise, one of which is destined for the innocent children. As for the last, the true Paradise, it is again divided into eight gardens, each of which has a hundred parts so that each of the faithful can enjoy the fruits of his actions appropriately. The Turkish mystic Ibrahim Hakki Erzerumlu, whose *Marifetname* is a most important source for our knowledge of Turkish folklore and mysticism in the eighteenth century, has described Paradise as an eight-storey pyramid—strangely enough, the multi-storey Christmas pyramids formerly built in the German Erzgebirge were also called 'paradises'.

Most philosophers did not accept verbatim the ideas of resurrection of the flesh and of a sensual Paradise and Hell. Mystics, too, refrained from such descriptions, or used them as allegories which might lead to Reality. The central experience they hoped for when thinking of Paradise was *ru'yā*, the beatific vision, as they understood it from Sura 75:22. Of course, the concept of *ru'yā* played an important rôle in early theological discussions, for the Mu'tazilites refused the possibility of a real vision of God. The Sufis regarded Paradise and Hell as mere veils:

> Only those who do not know the sweetness of absolute renunciation run after the brocade and Riḍwān's silk,

says 'Urfī in sixteenth-century India, referring to the famous story of Rābi'a al-'Adawiyya who was seen in her home town Basra some time in the eighth century, carrying a ewer with water in one hand and a burning torch in the other hand in order to put fire in Paradise and pour water into Hell, so that these two veils would disappear from the eyes of mankind and God would be worshipped for his own sake, not out of fear or hope. This legend reached Europe through Joinville in the early fourteenth century, and was retold in *Carité ou la vraie charité* by the French Quietist Camus in 1640. It has also appeared in modern German literature (Max Mell, *Die schönen Hände*).

> When He keeps you busy with Paradise and houris,
> know that He keeps you away from Himself ('Aṭṭār).

What is one to do with a couple of castles and some houris who are already several thousand years old? This was Yūnus Emre's question. In nineteenth-century India Ghālib harked back to this topic in his *Urdu Divan*:

> If Paradise is that which the Molla praises,
> then it is for us, who have lost ourselves, only a withered
> rose bouquet in the niche of forgetfulness!

A withered bouquet of roses! A hundred years before his compatriot Ghālib, Mīr Dard had sung:

> O ascetic! You may pluck roses in the meadows of paradise—
> For us, the smiling of our beloved is our paradise!

—a verse which alludes to the Prophetic tradition that the faithful will see his Lord smiling (*wa rabbuka ḍāḥik*).

The Paradise for which the mystic longed is the permanent

presence of God. No one has expressed this idea more beautifully and at the same time more simply than Yūnus Emre in his Turkish verse, which has become almost a folksong:

> The rivers all in Paradise
> Flow with the word Allah, Allah,
> And ev'ry longing nightingale
> He sings and sings Allah, Allah . . .

Everything—fragrance, growing, singing—is nothing but the most high name Allah. For the mystic, the real goal is the vision of God, 'a vision without the pain of seeing' (Iqbal), when he is completely surrounded by the divine light and experiences union with God in an inexplicable way as 'bliss unspeakable'.

The Islamic peoples do not call the memorial of a saint's death *'urs*, 'wedding', by accident for, as Yaḥyā ibn Mu'ādh says, 'Death is beautiful, because it leads the lover to his beloved'. The gallows became the bridal bed for Hallaj, the martyr mystic, as mystical poets of the eastern Islamic countries have often repeated:

> Do not complain: 'Separation, separation!' when you carry me to my tomb,
> because there is a blessed arrival behind the curtain for me. (Rūmī)

Such a 'spiritual marriage', however, can be experienced only when man prepares himself throughout his whole life for this last moment. It seems that the favorite *ḥadīth* of the mystics has to find its place here: *mūtū qabla an tamūtū*, 'Die before you die!' This means that man should die from his own lowly qualities and attain by *fanā*, 'annihilation', the divine Now in order to participate in an eternal life that is already here. This idea is an exact equivalent of the gnomic couplet of the German mystic poet Angelus Silesius:

> Ich selbst bin Ewigkeit, wenn ich die Zeit verlasse
> Und mich in Gott und Gott in mir zusammenfasse.

> I am eternity, when from time I rise,
> and myself in God, God in myself comprise.

In mystical terminology one might say that the voice of the Prophet who brings the Koran, or the voice of the perfected mystical leader whose heart is united with the *ḥaqīqa muḥammadiyya* (the spiritual principle of Muḥammad), and who calls the souls to this experience, is comparable to the trumpet of Isrāfīl, which announces resurrection. Meditation on the Koran plays an important rôle here: as the uncreated divine word, it establishes man's direct contact with God. The Shirazian mystic Rūzbihān Baqlī (d. 1209) has said:

> The Koran *is* the resurrection, for in it there are signs of the Divine Lordship . . . Everyone who knows the Koran is, so to speak, in the resurrection. What the Koran announces can be seen in a certain way with one's own eyes.

After the faithful one has experienced *fanā*, the state of *baqā*, or remaining in God, may follow, a state which is reached only fragmentarily in this world. This remaining in God, or duration, is not, however, a fixed and static state. Hope of *baqā* or 'eternal life' in Islam cannot be compared to the longing of the Hindu or the Buddhist to escape the painful eternal circles of rebirth, *samsāra*, in the immovable *nirvāna*; it is rather 'growing without diminishing', as Iqbal says at the end of the *Jāvīdnāme* (1932). Ghazzālī, in his *Iḥyā 'ulūm ad-dīn*, has talked about the eternity of longing, for longing grows stronger the deeper man dives into the abyss of divine life. God is infinite and cannot be traversed by any created being.

> In the sanctuary of love, resurrection is only the first resting place,

says 'Urfī, taking up Maulānā Rūmī's ideas. For 'when the journey to God is finished, the journey in God begins'. Thus 'Aṭṭār who, following Sanā'ī and preparing the way for Rūmī, was well-acquainted with this never-ending dive into the depths of the Divine, and has voiced the silent longing for God that permeates the world and can be detected in everything created, from stone to angel.

The eternal life that was the ideal of the mystics and their modern successors is not static. They take their inspiration from the fact that the Koran speaks of *daraja*, 'stairs', or 'levels', when mentioning Paradise. 'Heaven is no holiday', as Iqbal, the modern interpreter of this theory, has said. Eternal life is participation in the intensive infinity of God. Meister Eckhart had expressed similar views six hundred years ago:

> The depths of God cannot be plumbed, and deification may go as far as it wishes, but it can never reach the end.

The hope of a development of the soul after death, so clearly expressed in Iqbal's theology, is also found in Goethe, who discussed with Eckermann the necessity of constantly new activities even after death. It occurs in the works of some contemporary Christian philosophers of religion, such as Heinrich Scholz. Perhaps the most explicit statement in this respect was made by the Swedish Islamologist, Bishop Tor Andrae, in *The Last Things* (1937), where he sees the true meaning of eternal life as constant development:

> If the future life is real life, then it cannot be a life that is forever closed, completed and perfected. To live means to grow. To live means that in every moment something new, something that nobody could imagine or foresee may emerge from the eternal abysses of the fountain of life.

The Islamic mystics and poets have expressed similar ideas throughout the centuries. By interiorizing death and resurrection, by constant growth through sacrifice, man can obey the order that was given to him at the beginning of creation: that is, to bear witness to God's unity and surrender to his will. He can thus experience God who is Creator, Sustainer, and Judge but who is also called the Merciful, and in whose hands man's destiny is kept. In this perfect surrender, he may even forget the horrors of the Last Judgment and feel happy in the hope of meeting his Lord and Friend. Iqbal's verses about the faithful, written shortly before his own death, are an appropriate expression of what a faithful Muslim feels when confronted with the problem of creation and Judgment:

> In the hem of his night there is dawn,
> From his star the radiance of the world shines forth.
> How else could I describe the faithful believer?
> He smiles when death approaches him.

Select Bibliography

A. Asin Palacios, *La escatologia musulmana en la Divina Comedia* (Madrid, 1919; 2nd ed., 1943).

D. S. Attema, *De mohammedaansche opvattingen omtrent het tijdstrip van den Jongsten Dag en zijn voortekenen* (Amsterdam, 1942).

Carra de Vaux, *Fragments d'eschatologie musulmane* (Brussels, 1895).

W. Eickmann, *Die Angelologie und Dämonologie des Korans im Vergleich zu der Engel- und Geisterlehre der Heiligen Schrift* (New York & Leipzig, 1908).

R. Eklund, *Life between Death and Resurrection according to Islam* (Uppsala, 1941).

al-Ghazzālī, *ad-durra al-fākkhira*; German translation by M. Brugsch, *Die kostbare Perle im Wissen des Jenseits* (Hannover, 1923; *id. Iḥyā ᶜulūm ad-dīn,* (Bulaq, 1298h/1872 and often); a survey of its contents: G.-H. Bousquet, *Ih'yā ᶜouloum ad-dīn, ou vivification des sciences de la foi* (Paris, 1955).

J. Horovitz, *Das koranische Paradies* (Jerusalem, 1923).

T. Huitema, *De voorspraak (shafāᶜa) in den Islam* (Leiden, 1936).

E. Lehmann-J. Pedersen: 'Der Beweis für die Auferstehung im Koran', in *Der: Islam*, V (1915).

R. Leszinski, *Muhammadanische Traditionen über das Jüngste Gericht* (Heidelberg, 1909).

J. Macdonald: 'Islamic Eschatology I: the creation of man and angels in the eschatological literature', in: *Islamic Studies,* 3/3 (Karachi, 1964).

L. Massignon, 'Die Auferstehung in der mohammedanischen Welt', in: *Eranos-Jahrbuch*, 6 (1939).

Jonas Meyer, *Die Hölle im Islam* (Diss., Basle, 1901).

SELECT BIBLIOGRAPHY

A. Schimmel, 'The Celestial Garden in Islam', in: *The Islamic Garden,* ed. R. Ettinghausen (Dumbarton Oaks, Washington, D.C., 1976).

T. O'Shaughnessy, *Muhammad's Thoughts on Death* (Leiden, 1969).

A. J. Wensinck, *The Muslim Creed* (Cambridge, 1932, repr. 1955).

M. Wolff, *Muhammadanische Eschatologie* (Leipzig, 1872).

The articles *djanna, djahannam, al-ḳiyāma, Munkar and Nakīr, shafāᶜa* in the *Smaller Encyclopedia of Islam.* Every study of Muslim theology and mysticism contains some information on eschatological problems.

Authors

Peter *Antes*, Professor of the History of Religions, Pädagogische Hochschule Niedersachsen, Hanover, Federal Republic of Germany.

Smail *Balić*, Head Librarian of the National Library, Vienna, Austria.

Josef *Blank*, Professor of New Testament Studies, University of Saarbrücken, Federal Republic of Germany.

Horst *Bürkle*, Head of Department of Religious Studies and Missiology in the Faculty of Protestant Theology, Munich University, Federal Republic of Germany.

Abdoldjavad *Falatūri*, Professor of Islamology and Philosophy, University of Cologne, Federal Republic of Germany.

Richard *Gramlich*, Professor of the History of Religions, University of Freiburg, Federal Republic of Germany.

Rudi *Paret*, Professor Emeritus of Islamic Studies, University of Tübingen, Federal Republic of Germany.

Annemarie *Schimmel*, Professor of Indo-Muslim Culture, Harvard University, Cambridge, Mass., USA.

Raymund *Schwager*, Co-Editor of the journal *Orientierung*, Zürich, Switzerland.